Carbs & Cals SMOOTHIES

80 healthy smoothie recipes & 275 photos of ingredients to create your own!

1ST EDITION

First published in Great Britain in 2016
by Chello Publishing Limited
Registered Company Number 7237986
www.chellopublishing.co.uk | info@chellopublishing.co.uk

With special thanks to: Alan Gray, Badger Brown, Basma Gale, Fran Turner, Fran Unerman, George Malache, Georgie Williams, Hannah Rowland, Jon Gibson, Justine Rose, Kerry Lee Watson, Marina Popova, Matt Hippisley, Maxine Gregory, Myles Barry Jackson, Nia Lynn, Racer Cartlidge, Richard Ashby, Salim Balolia, Simon Callaghan, Stu McMillan, Tom Gale, Vic Francis, Yoshi Balolia, Zoë Nattress.

The information contained in this book is not a substitute for medical or other professional guidance. Please consult your GP before making any alterations to medications or changing medical treatment. Although all reasonable care has been taken in the writing of this book, the authors and publisher are not responsible for any specific health needs; they do not accept any legal responsibility or liability for any personal injury or other consequences, damage or loss arising from any use of information and advice contained within this book.

The authors have asserted their moral rights.

ISBN: 978-1-908261-11-3 Printed in Malta 0217

Authors	Chris Cheyette BSc (Hons) MSc RD
	Yello Balolia BA (Hons)
Recipes by	Chris Cheyette BSc (Hons) MSc RD
	Yello Balolia BA (Hons)
Photography	Simon Callaghan & Francesca Turner
Retouching	George F Malache & Iulian Diaconu
Page & Cover Design	George F Malache
Additional Layout	Maxine Gregory BA (Hons)
	Yello Balolia BA (Hons)
Introduction Text	Victoria Francis BSc (Hons) RD

For more information, please visit:
www.carbsandcals.com

Contents

Introduction 4
Ingredient health benefits 12
Smoothies as part of your diet plan 16
How to use this book 19
Guide to making smoothies 24

Smoothie Recipes 28
Low-Calorie Smoothies 28
General Smoothies 38
5-a-day Smoothies 78
High-Fibre Smoothies 88
High-Protein Smoothies 98

Smoothie Ingredients 108
Cereals 108
Dried Fruit 109
Fruit 112
Frozen Fruit 123
Herbs 125
Juice 126
Liquids 130
Milk 131
Nuts & Seeds 134
Powders 139
Spreads & Sauces 141
Vegetables & Pulses 143
Yogurt 155

Index 156
Smoothies Index 156
Ingredients Index 157

About the Authors / Awards 160

Introduction

In recent years, juicing and smoothies have become a popular movement among many health-conscious people. Many advocates of juicing and smoothies encourage beliefs that such products can help detoxify, cleanse our bodies or help with anti-ageing. From a scientific point of view, such claims are not evidence-based and can be misleading. Commercial juices and smoothies are often sensationalised and promoted as a healthy option and a weight loss tool; "Shake your smoothie and you already start to feel healthy!". They are marketed as nutritious, virtuous and necessary for clean, healthy living, but many of these commercially-produced smoothies are high in sugar and calories, and can contain a variety of additives and preservatives.

So do smoothies have a place in your diet? Absolutely! Homemade smoothies can play a valuable role in contributing to your overall health. By making smoothies yourself, you can control the contents, be more mindful of what you consume, and reduce the number of additives and preservatives by using fresh fruit and vegetables.

This book aims to visually show you how to make your own nutrient-rich smoothies, to be enjoyed as part of a healthy, balanced diet. It does not intend to give you any false hope or suggest that drinking a smoothie will help you live longer. By providing you with evidence-based nutrition facts and recipes, the book will inspire and help you to reach your nutrition goals; be it to simply meet your 5-a-day, increase fibre intake, start the day with a healthy breakfast or achieve your weight loss target.

What is the difference between blending and juicing?

A smoothie involves blending pieces of fruit and vegetables together with a base such as water, fruit juice, milk or yogurt; the consistency of the resulting drink may range from very thick to quite watery, depending on the chosen ingredients. The whole food is used (minus inedible pips and skin), retaining all the nutrients, and because they can be made with protein sources, they can be an energy-rich meal replacement or simply a nutrient and antioxidant boost.

Juicing is the process of extracting the liquid content of whole foods through a juicing machine. The pulp left behind is indigestible material such as the skin, seeds or pith (containing fibre amongst other nutrients), which is then discarded. For this reason, juices are low in fibre and protein. However, a 150ml portion can still contribute towards one of your 5-a-day and can also provide a valuable source of vitamins and antioxidants. Compared to a smoothie, juices are more likely to raise your blood glucose rapidly and may leave you feeling hungry soon afterwards, due to the lack of fibre and protein.

Health benefits of smoothies

Reach your 5-a-day

Scientific evidence strongly supports the role of fruit and vegetables in reducing the risk of certain illnesses, such as heart disease and cancer. Current UK dietary advice is to consume at least 5 portions of fruit and vegetables a day, a recommendation that is supported by the World Health Organisation, who recommend at least 400g fruit and vegetables per day. This amount is actually the minimum and yet research shows only 2 out of 3 adults meet these recommendations.

The following count as 1 portion of your 5-a-day: 80g fresh, frozen or tinned fruit and veg; 30g dried fruit; 150ml pure, unsweetened fruit or vegetable juice; 80g beans and pulses.

3½
5-a-day

Page
50

6
5-a-day

Page
87

A recent study found that only 4% of children eat fruit with their breakfast. This rose to 45% when the school offered them a smoothie. So smoothies can boost your fruit and vegetable intake and help achieve your 5-a-day whilst also introducing some fruits and vegetables that you may not ordinarily eat alone, such as kale, spinach or beetroot. Using a rainbow of fruits and vegetables in your smoothies will provide a wide variety of nutrients including vitamin C, beta carotene, phytonutrients and antioxidants, all of which nourish your body and reduce the risk of health problems.

Government guidelines make a recommendation that commercial smoothies should only count up to a maximum of 2 of your 5-a-day, as many commercial smoothies are filtered or sieved which means it is common that some of the fibre is removed. Homemade smoothies, using the whole fruit and vegetable in sufficient quantities, can contribute to more than 2 of your 5-a-day. This book contains 10 smoothie recipes that contain all 5 of your 5-a-day (see pages 78 to 87) and even one smoothie with 6 portions of fruit & veg! But don't stop there; remember 5 portions is the minimum and you will certainly benefit from exceeding this target.

Raspberries 80g

1
5-a-day

Cucumber 40g

1/2
5-a-day

Increase your fibre intake

There is strong evidence that an increase in our total dietary fibre intake (especially cereal grains and whole grains) is associated with a lower risk of heart disease, type 2 diabetes and bowel cancer. Soluble fibre found in fruit and vegetables is also known to slow down digestion (helping us to feel full for longer), lower cholesterol and play a role in controlling blood sugar levels. These benefits have led the Scientific Advisory Committee on Nutrition to update fibre recommendations to 30g per day for adults (current average intake is 18g per day). With an average portion of fruit containing 1-3g fibre, smoothies can play an important role in boosting your fibre intake and promoting good bowel health. The addition of oats or nut butters will further boost the fibre content.

4g Fibre

Apple Rings 30g

3g Fibre

Mango 80g

8g Fibre

Page 96

10g Fibre

Page 88

Boost your sources of protein and bone-building calcium

Using a base such as milk or yogurt provides a good source of lean protein, known to keep you feeling satisfied until your next meal. Other protein-rich sources, including nut butters or seeds, can also be added to boost protein intake and help stabilise blood sugar levels. Coconut or almond milk can be used for variation of taste, although be aware that these non-dairy milks are lower in protein. Soya milk contains almost as much protein as cow's milk, so is a good substitute for those avoiding dairy. Using low-fat dairy sources such as yogurt or milk also provides a valuable source of calcium, which is needed for good bone health.

Almonds 20g

4g
Protein

Greek Yogurt 100g

7g
Protein

10g
Protein

Page
98

15g
Protein

Page
104

Grab a quick breakfast on the move

With our fast-paced lifestyles, breakfast can be easily forgotten or pushed down our list of priorities, despite the overwhelming evidence showing those who consume breakfast are more likely to be a healthy weight, have balanced diets and function better. Smoothies are an easy, quick and nutritious breakfast choice and a great way to boost your hydration at the start of the day.

150 Cals — Page 61

255 Cals — Page 75

260 Cals — Page 101

Refuel your energy needs after a workout

There is a lot of controversy over what to use to refuel after a workout. The two key ingredients to help you recover are carbohydrates (for energy) and protein (repair and growth of muscle cells). A protein-packed smoothie is a great choice to refuel your muscles whilst keeping you hydrated at the same time.

31g Carbs — 9g Protein — Page 91

37g Carbs — 11g Protein — Page 103

38g Carbs — 14g Protein — Page 105

What is a healthy, balanced diet and how can smoothies be included?

The benefits of a healthy, balanced diet include a reduced risk of long term conditions such as cancer and heart disease, help with weight maintenance and improvement in general health and well-being.

Within our diet there are 5 main food groups. The Department of Health's Eatwell Plate shows the proportions of the 5 different food groups, including snacks, that we should eat and drink each day to ensure we meet our nutritional requirements. A healthy, balanced diet contains a variety of foods from these food groups to provide the following nutrients:

- ★ Antioxidants, vitamins and minerals from fruit and vegetables
- ★ Calcium from dairy foods such as milk and yogurt
- ★ B-vitamins and fibre from wholegrain, starchy carbs such as oats, pasta and bread
- ★ Protein from meat, fish, nuts and eggs
- ★ Omega 3 oils from oily fish and nuts

Smoothies contribute towards a healthy, balanced diet as they contain nutrient-dense foods, such as fruit and vegetables, wholegrain cereals and low-fat dairy products, all of which are in the Eatwell plate.

The eatwell plate

Use the eatwell plate to help you get the balance right. It shows how much of what you eat should come from each food group.

FOOD STANDARDS AGENCY

eatwell.gov.uk

For more information on healthy eating and 5-a-day, visit:
www.carbsandcals.com

Ingredient Health Benefits

Banana
Elevate your mood by eating a tryptophan-rich banana

Cherries
Thought to raise melatonin levels and aid a good night's sleep

Dried Apricots
Great non-dairy source of calcium, needed for bone and dental health

Grapefruit
Promotes a healthy immune system, thanks to its vitamin C content

Pineapple
High in manganese, which helps with energy production in the body

Blueberries
An excellent source of cancer-fighting antioxidants

Dates
High potassium content, which regulates heartbeat and blood pressure

Figs
Contain prebiotics to promote a healthy digestive system

Mango
Contains immune-boosting vitamin A

Plums
Rich in polyphenols, which are protective against heart disease

Strawberries
High in vitamin C and antioxidants to protect against cancer

Please note: these benefits must be taken in context of eating a wide variety of foods in your diet and no single ingredient is a 'superfood'.

Avocado

Rich in omega 3 fats, which are thought to play a role in preventing dementia

Beetroot

High in potassium, lowering blood pressure

Broccoli

High in vitamin K, which is needed for wound healing

Carrots

Protect your eyes and help with vision in dim light, due to their high vitamin A content

Ginger

Known to alleviate discomfort and pain in the stomach

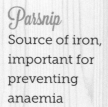

Kale

A source of folate, needed for healthy blood and brain function

Parsnip

Source of iron, important for preventing anaemia

Red Cabbage

High in vitamin K, for maintaining bone strength and health

Spinach

Rich in magnesium, which helps to calm the body and relax muscles

Sweet Potato

Fibre-rich and a source of slow releasing energy

Tomato

Contains lycopene, an antioxidant known to protect against heart disease

Yellow Pepper

High in beta carotene (which makes vitamin A) to avoid an itchy scalp and dry hair

Almonds
Heart-healthy due to their high vitamin E content

Brazil Nuts
Rich source of selenium, a trace element that plays an important role in the immune system

Cashews
Good source of zinc, essential for enhancing memory and thinking skills

Hazelnuts
The high vitamin E content makes these great for healthy skin

Pecans
High in protein and fibre to fill you up and prevent snacking

Walnuts
Anti-inflammatory, so great for those suffering with joint pain and arthritis

Chia Seeds
High in fibre and an excellent source of protein for vegans and vegetarians

Hemp Seeds
Good source of magnesium, which is needed for healthy bones and teeth

Linseeds
Source of gluten/wheat-free fibre for bowel health

Mixed Seeds
Keep brain function in tip-top health with a boost of omega 3 fatty acids

Pumpkin Seeds
Keep hair and skin looking healthy, thanks to their rich iodine content

Sunflower Seeds
Rich in magnesium, which is thought to play a protective role against type 2 diabetes

Coconut Water

Great for hydrating, as it contains potassium and sodium

Natural Yogurt

Contains probiotics to support a healthy digestive system

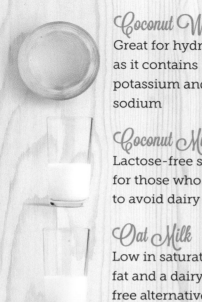

Coconut Milk

Lactose-free so great for those who need to avoid dairy

Milk

Great source of bone-strengthening calcium and B2, which is needed for healthy skin and eyes

Oat Milk

Low in saturated fat and a dairy-free alternative to cow's milk

Soya Milk

Rich in soluble fibre and isoflavones, both of which keep the heart healthy

Cacao

High in potassium, which regulates heartbeat and blood pressure

Muesli

Good source of carbohydrate for energy

Spirulina

Contains a range of B vitamins, needed for maximum energy conversion from foods

Oat Bran

Soluble fibre found in oat bran can help with weight maintenance and lower cholesterol

Wheatgrass

Contains antioxidants to help fight the ageing process

Oats

Provide a slow release of energy to prevent slumps in concentration

Smoothies as part of your diet plan

Different diets work for different people. The key to achieving success involves finding the right diet plan that works for you and your lifestyle, and one you can stick to. Smoothies offer a low-calorie, nutrient-rich option to include within many diet plans such as:

5:2 diet

A high-protein smoothie is a perfect meal replacement to keep you feeling satisfied until your next meal. It is also a quick and easy way to reach your 5-a-day on fasting days. Our "Melon Salad" smoothie has only 90 calories, but 7g fibre and 7g protein, making it a perfect breakfast or evening meal replacement, still leaving you with 411 calories to play with for the rest of your day. For more information about the 5:2 diet see our 5:2 Diet Photos book.

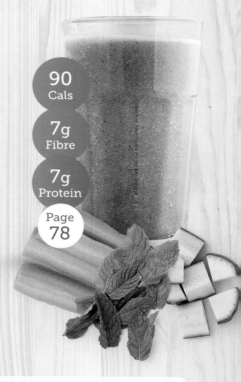

90 Cals

7g Fibre

7g Protein

Page **78**

5:2 Diet Photos
To buy your copy, visit:
www.carbsandcals.com/5-2

Low-carb diets

These are popular amongst many people who want to lose weight and also those with diabetes who manage their blood glucose levels. Smoothies with a low-carb base such as almond milk, water or coconut water and predominantly vegetables will be a quick and simple low-carb snack. For example, our "Pick up a Pepper" smoothie has only 12g carbs.

12g Carbs

Page **53**

High-protein diets

These are based on the principle that protein is the nutrient that keeps us feeling full for longer and has minimal impact on blood glucose levels. Smoothie recipes in this book use fibre-rich protein sources including nuts and seeds, and low-fat protein sources such as milk and yogurt. Research has shown that our bodies are unable to utilise much more than 20g protein at one time. Our protein-rich "Morning Glory" smoothie provides 17g protein and 12g fibre; a perfect breakfast choice to keep you feeling satisfied and energised until lunch!

17g Protein

Page **106**

High-fibre

The average UK adult currently consumes 18g fibre per day, so for many it will seem a tall order to reach the new recommendation of 30g per day. Choosing our "Fruit Pod" smoothie for a mid-morning snack will provide a third of your daily fibre requirements for only 130 calories!

10g Fibre

Page **88**

Smoothies for people with type 1 and type 2 diabetes

Diabetes is a condition in which glucose levels in the blood are too high because the body cannot use the glucose properly. The two main types of diabetes are type 1 and type 2. Type 1 diabetes develops because the immune system attacks and destroys the cells that produce insulin, which leads to high blood glucose levels. Treatment is administration of insulin via injections or pump. Type 2 diabetes develops when the pancreas does not produce enough insulin, or the body is unable to use the insulin effectively (known as insulin resistance). Type 2 diabetes can primarily be treated with a healthy diet and lifestyle changes, such as increased physical activity. However, it is a progressive condition and therefore many people may need to commence diabetes medication at some point, to control their blood glucose levels.

For people with type 1 diabetes who adjust their insulin dose according to their carb intake, smoothies can be included in their diet as long as the carb content of the smoothie is calculated and matched with quick-acting insulin. Vegetables, protein foods and some of the smoothie bases will not need to be counted, whereas the fruit, milks, cereals and some of the sauces (such as maple syrup) will need to be counted. For ease of use, each smoothie recipe in this book clearly shows its carb content.

For overweight or obese people with type 2 diabetes, weight loss is the primary strategy to control blood glucose levels. As already shown, smoothies can be included as part of a weight loss programme. If you have diabetes and are taking medication (including insulin), speak with your healthcare professional for guidance on how to include smoothies in your daily diet.

How to use this book

Using the recipes

This book includes 80 carefully-crafted smoothie recipes, divided into the following sections:

Low-calorie
50 cals or less
Pages **28 - 37**

5-a-day
All 5 of your 5-a-day!
Pages **78 - 87**

35 Cals

150 Cals

5 5-a-day

9g Fibre

12g Protein

General recipes
Pages **38 - 77**

High-fibre
8g fibre or more
Pages **88 - 97**

High-protein
10g protein or more
Pages **98 - 107**

Within each section, the smoothies are listed in calorie order, starting with the lowest calorie recipe. For each smoothie, the nutritional information for the following nutrients are clearly displayed in colour-coded circles:

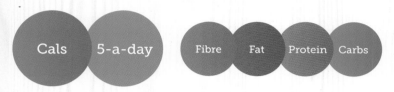

Cals 5-a-day   Fibre Fat Protein Carbs

Simply browse the selection of recipes and select ones that are suitable for your dietary needs. Try a variety of smoothies that meet your requirements to find your favourites, and make a note of these.

A few things to note:

★ Recipes in the book use average/medium sizes of fruit & veg, and weights shown are for the edible part (after being peeled or destoned), unless otherwise stated.

★ Some recipes use a handy measure (e.g. "handful of spinach") instead of a specific weight. Should you wish to know the exact weights, simply find that portion in the ingredients section. For example, the "Hey Pesto!" recipe on page 31 uses "2 handfuls Kale". Looking at Kale on page 149, you will see that 2 handfuls weigh 40g.

★ Garnishes shown in the photos are for decoration only and are not included in the nutritional information.

Kale
40g, 2 handfuls

1g Protein

1g Fat

2g Fibre

1g Carbs

13 Cals

½ 5-a-day

Creating your own recipes

The potential smoothie combinations are endless, so why not get creative? Try making up your own from the list of ingredients at the back of this book (pages 108 to 155). The nutritional content of each individual ingredient is shown, giving you the flexibility to create smoothie recipes to meet your own personal dietary goal. Again, it's worth writing down the details of your creations so you have a record of nutritional information and can make the recipe again in future. For a practical guide on how to make smoothies, see pages 24 to 27.

0g Protein
0g Fat
2g Fibre

Apple
80g, ½ medium

9g Carbs
38 Cals
1 5-a-day

0g Protein
0g Fat
2g Fibre

Pear
80g, cored

8g Carbs
32 Cals
1 5-a-day

0g Protein
0g Fat
1g Fibre

Lime
10g, ⅛ with skin

1g Carbs
3 Cals
0 5-a-day

My Smoothie
Apple 80g (38 cals)
Pear 80g (32 cals)
Lime 10g (3 cals)
Water & Ice
TOTAL = 73 cals

Making a 5:2 diet meal plan

The 5:2 approach enables you to lose weight without constant deprivation. Eating a normal, healthy diet 5 days a week, and fasting on the 2 remaining days, reduces your overall calorie intake and has proven to be an effective method for many people.

Here is an example of how to include a smoothie into your fasting day:

1. Decide how you would like to split your calorie allowance for the day. For example your 500 calories could be made up of:
   ★ 200 cals for breakfast
   ★ 75 cals for a snack
   ★ 225 cals for dinner

2. Decide which meals or snacks you wish to substitute with smoothies.

3. Browse this book and decide which smoothie fits your calorie needs. For example, a 200 calorie, protein-rich smoothie for breakfast to keep you feeling satisfied for longer, or a 75 calorie pick-me-up smoothie snack.

4. Use this alongside our 5:2 Diet Photos book to make your fasting days feel like a feast not a famine!

To buy your copy, visit: www.carbsandcals.com/5-2

Daily meal plan:

Breakfast:

195 Cals

Page **99**

Daytime snack:

75 Cals

Page **40**

Evening meal:

235 Cals

Prawn stir-fry from 5:2 Diet Photos book

Total cals: **505** Cals **8½** 5-a-day

Producing a meal plan for a 1,500 calorie diet

Fad diets which usually promise quick weight loss results are hard to follow, often limiting in nutrients and offer little benefit in the long term. For many, weight re-gain is common once a normal diet is resumed. Following a 1,500 calorie diet plan should help you lose around ½ kg (1lb) a week (more if you have lots to lose), without feeling you are depriving yourself of everything!

375
Cals

Page
106

A smoothie is a great way to ensure you meet your nutrient needs whilst limiting your calorie intake, either as a meal replacement or a low-calorie snack.

An example of a daily meal plan looks like this:

Breakfast	290 cals	1 slice wholegrain toast, topped with 2 eggs (scrambled with 1 tbsp skimmed milk), served with grilled mushrooms and tomato
Snack	185 cals	30g unsalted almonds
Lunch	375 cals	"Morning Glory" smoothie (page 106)
Snack	140 cals	Skinny cappuccino and digestive biscuit
Dinner	480 cals	Salmon skewers with Moroccan couscous and roasted vegetables
Total	1,470 cals	

For info on weight loss and how to work out your calorie target, visit:
www.carbsandcals.com/BMI

Guide to making Smoothies

For those new to blending, the next few pages offer some important information on what to look for in a blender, tips for buying ingredients, and the practicalities of making smoothies.

What should I look for in a blender?

There are many new blenders hitting the market, each with their own health claim, which can leave consumers quite confused! The large variety of brands, models, types and features (which you may or may not need!) can send you into a head-spin. Newer models are often marketed as personal blenders, with a simple cup that is used to make and then drink the smoothie; perfect when on the go.

Some important features you may want to consider when choosing a blender include:

★ Power of at least 500 watts
★ Ice-crushing blade - for blending/crushing ice
★ Variable speeds with a pulse function
★ Stainless steel blade assembly
★ Direct drive motor operation for durability
★ Easy removal of blade assembly for cleaning
★ Capacity (if making smoothies for more than 1 person)

Most brands of blenders have a number of different models, each varying in size, function and cost.

To see our recommended smoothie blenders, please visit:
www.carbsandcals.com/blenders

Things to note when buying ingredients

★ Always use fresh, ripe fruit & veg

★ Aim to buy organic produce where possible

★ When buying tinned fruit, choose 'tinned in juice' varieties, rather than 'tinned in syrup', and drain the juice away

★ Use 100% coconut water, as some brands can be full of sugar

★ To keep the cost of your smoothie down, choose fruit and vegetables that are in season as these are often on offer

★ Frozen fruit tends to be less expensive than fresh

★ Buying your dry ingredients in bulk is a great way of saving money too

★ A great way to add variety and ensure you always have your smoothie ingredients to hand is to order a fruit and vegetable box. Each delivery is different so you never know what smoothie recipe will be on the menu!

To see our recommended veg box companies, please visit:
www.carbsandcals.com/vegbox

The practicalities of blending

1 Insert the blades into your blender before the ingredients

2 When recipes include leafy greens (such as spinach or kale), put these into the blender first so they're not left floating at the top or stuck in the lid

3 Remove pips and stones from produce (e.g. plum and apricot stones), to avoid damaging the blades

4 Experiment with the size of fruit & vegetable chunks until you find the size that your particular blender can handle

5 It's important to add liquid to your blender, as this will prevent the blades from getting damaged

6 To measure out liquids like water, milk or juice, you can use your scales instead of a measuring jug (120ml milk = 120g milk)

7 Always add ice last, so it doesn't melt too quickly

8 · · · · · · · Frozen fruit can be used in
place of fresh fruit, to cool your
smoothies instead of using ice

9 Always leave room for expansion
- at least one third capacity

10 Never operate the blender without the lid;
even the smallest amount of food can create
quite a mess if the lid is not applied!

11 Even if the lid appears a snug fit, hold the lid whilst blending

12 Increase the speed of your blender in stages,
to ensure the smoothie blends evenly

13 If food sticks, stop the blender and use a rubber
spatula to move food down to the blades

14 If your smoothie is too thick and you would like it to be a thinner
consistency, simply add more water or more of the liquid
base, e.g. almond milk (but remember, any extra liquid added
other than water will alter the calorie and nutrient content)

15 Similarly, adding more ice to your
smoothie will make it colder · · · · ·

16 Your blender is your friend;
get to know its behaviour so
you can make smoothies as
quickly and easily as possible!

17 It is recommended to drink smoothies within 15
minutes of making them, since many ingredients will
begin to oxidise once they've been blended

Acid Raspberries

Our lowest-calorie smoothie; quench your thirst for only 35 cals

Ingredients

60g	**Frozen Raspberries**
¼	**Lime** (with skin)
250ml	**Water**

35 Cals

1 5-a-day

4g Fibre

0g Fat

1g Protein

7g Carbs

Size
Medium
330g

Recipe Tip
Alternatively, use fresh raspberries
but add ice to keep the smoothie cool

Cucumelon Rose

This 45 cal smoothie provides 3 of your 5-a-day

Ingredients

80g	Cantaloupe Melon
80g	Galia Melon
¼	Cucumber
1 tsp	Rose Water
100ml	Water
3	Ice Cubes

9g Carbs

1g Protein

0g Fat

2g Fibre

3 5-a-day

45 Cals

Recipe Tip

Leave out the rose water if not available

Size
Medium
385g

Blue Ginger

A zingy spin on the classic lemon & ginger combo

Ingredients

60g	**Blueberries**
1 inch	**Ginger** (peeled)
¼	**Lemon** (juice only)
¼	**Lime** (juice only)
140ml	Water
6	Ice Cubes

45 Cals

1 5-a-day

1g Fibre

0g Fat

1g Protein

9g Carbs

Size
Medium
310g

Nutrition Fact
Blueberries are an excellent source of
cancer-fighting antioxidants

Hey Pesto!

This extreme-green, savoury delight is our lowest-carb smoothie

Ingredients

½	**Celery** stalk
⅙	**Courgette**
⅛	**Cucumber**
2	handfuls **Kale**
1	large handful **Lambs Lettuce**
2	handfuls **Spinach**
6	**Basil** leaves
½	**Lemon** (juice only)
80ml	Water
5	Ice Cubes

4g Carbs

4g Protein

1g Fat

4g Fibre

3 5-a-day

45 Cals

Nutrition Fact
Spinach is rich in magnesium, which helps to calm the body and relax muscles

Size
Medium
395g

Pear of Blueberries

Light and floaty, this is more like a juice than a smoothie

Ingredients

40g	Blueberries
¼	Pear (cored)
⅛	Lime (with skin)
¼	Lime (juice only)
200ml	Water
6	Ice Cubes

45 Cals

1 5-a-day

3g Fibre

0g Fat

1g Protein

11g Carbs

Size
Medium
380g

Recipe Tip
Swap the pear for ¼ apple if you prefer

Melon Quencher

Refreshing and hydrating, like a tasty watermelon mojito

Ingredients

80g	**Galia Melon**
80g	**Watermelon**
5	**Mint** leaves
½	**Lime** (juice only)
140ml	Water
3	Ice Cubes

11g Carbs

1g Protein

0g Fat

1g Fibre

2 5-a-day

45 Cals

Recipe Tip

Honeydew or cantaloupe can be used instead of galia melon

Size

Medium
360g

Lychee Tea

A small cup of sweet green tea

Ingredients

3	**Lychees**
4	**Strawberries**
5	**Mint** leaves
100ml	**Green Tea** (cooled)
3	Ice Cubes

50 Cals

1½ 5-a-day

1g Fibre

0g Fat

1g Protein

12g Carbs

Size
Small
260g

Recipe Tip
Use tinned lychees (drained) if fresh
are not available

Grapefruit Froth

Like it tangy? Try this mouthwatering mixture of pineapple and citrus

Ingredients

80g	**Pineapple**
¼	**Red Grapefruit** (peeled)
120ml	Water
6	Ice Cubes

12g Carbs **1g** Protein **0g** Fat **2g** Fibre

1½ 5-a-day **50** Cals

Nutrition Fact
Grapefruit promotes a healthy immune system due to its vitamin C content

Size
Medium
340g

Watermelon Mary

A savoury blend of tomato, basil and watermelon

Ingredients

80g	**Watermelon**
1/8	**Cucumber**
3	**Tomatoes** (small)
6	**Basil** leaves
1/4	**Lemon** (juice only)
80ml	Water
3	Ice Cubes

50 Cals

2½ 5-a-day

2g Fibre

1g Fat

2g Protein

10g Carbs

Size
Medium
380g

Nutrition Fact
Tomatoes contain antioxidant lycopene,
known to protect against heart disease

Carrot & Cucumber Cooler

This light cooler is super simple to make

Ingredients

⅓	**Orange** (peeled)
½	**Carrot**
¼	**Cucumber**
100ml	Water
6	Ice Cubes

11g Carbs **2g** Protein **0g** Fat **4g** Fibre

2½ 5-a-day **50** Cals

Recipe Tip
Add some ginger for an extra zing!

Size
Medium
380g

Love it or Hate it!

This interesting combo of tomato and chocolate will leave you licking your lips or scrunching your face!

Ingredients

3	**Tomatoes** (small)
5g	**Dark Chocolate**
¼	**Lime** (juice only)
80ml	**Coconut Water**
3	Ice Cubes

60 Cals

1 5-a-day

2g Fibre

2g Fat

1g Protein

11g Carbs

Size
Small
255g

Recipe Tip
Use an organic dark chocolate variety with 70% cocoa content

Mango Tango

The name says it all!

Ingredients

¾	**Mango**
½	**Lime** (juice only)
180ml	Water
6	Ice Cubes

17g Carbs

1g Protein

0g Fat

4g Fibre

1 5-a-day

70 Cals

Recipe Tip

Swap the water for coconut water for an alternative taste (making it 100 cals)

Size
Medium
400g

Passionately Green

Cold and refreshing, this smoothie is thinner than it looks

Ingredients

½	**Mango**
1	**Passion Fruit** (flesh only)
2	handfuls **Kale**
140ml	Water
6	Ice Cubes

75 Cals

2 5-a-day

6g Fibre

1g Fat

3g Protein

14g Carbs

Size
Medium
380g

Nutrition Fact
Kale is a good source of folate, needed for healthy blood and brain function

Carrot Classic

This combination is a classic for a reason: it's delicious!

Ingredients

½	Red Apple
4	Strawberries
½	Carrot
½	Celery stalk
100ml	Water
5	Ice Cubes

18g Carbs **1g** Protein **0g** Fat **5g** Fibre

3 5-a-day **75** Cals

Nutrition Fact

Strawberries are high in vitamin C and antioxidants to protect against cancer

Size
Medium
400g

Tarty Blast

Lemon and lime juice provide a refreshing zing

Ingredients

2	**Kiwis** (peeled)
2 tsp	**Dried Goji Berries**
2	handfuls **Spinach**
5	**Mint** leaves
½	**Lemon** (juice only)
½	**Lime** (juice only)
100ml	Water
6	Ice Cubes

85 Cals

2 5-a-day

4g Fibre

1g Fat

3g Protein

16g Carbs

Size
Medium
385g

Recipe Tip
Add more or less mint, according
to your taste preference

Kale Kerfuffle

Cover your mouth in green with this apple and veg melange

Ingredients

1	**Green Apple** (small)
½	**Celery** stalk
⅙	**Courgette**
2	handfuls **Kale**
2	sprigs **Parsley**
¼	**Lemon** (juice only)
80ml	Water
6	Ice Cubes

17g Carbs

3g Protein

1g Fat

6g Fibre

2½ 5-a-day

85 Cals

Recipe Tip

Courgette can be replaced with cucumber if preferred

Size

Medium
430g

Citrus Rooter

This vibrant, 90 cal concoction contains 7g fibre and 3 of your 5-a-day

Ingredients

⅓	**Orange** (peeled)
1	**Carrot**
1 inch	**Ginger** (peeled)
1	**Raw Beetroot** (peeled)
100ml	Water
5	Ice Cubes

90 Cals

3 5-a-day

7g Fibre

0g Fat

3g Protein

20g Carbs

Size
Medium
405g

Nutrition Fact
Beetroot has been shown to lower blood pressure for people with hypertension

Cocopineapple Cooler

Light and creamy, like a cloud in a cup

Ingredients
100g **Frozen Pineapple**
240ml **Coconut Water**

| 23g Carbs | 1g Protein | 0g Fat | 1g Fibre |

| 1 5-a-day | 95 Cals |

Nutrition Fact
Coconut water is great for hydrating as it contains potassium and sodium

Size
Medium
340g

Orangetastic

Brighten up the dullest day with this colourful classic

Ingredients

⅓	**Orange** (peeled)	
½	**Red Apple**	
1	**Carrot**	
1 inch	**Ginger** (peeled)	
120ml	Water	
5	Ice Cubes	

100 Cals

3 5-a-day

6g Fibre

0g Fat

2g Protein

23g Carbs

Size
Medium
425g

Nutrition Fact
Carrots are high in vitamin A, which
protects your eyes and helps with vision

Speckled Melon

Not only is it pretty, it's also refreshing and super-hydrating

Ingredients

½ **Passion Fruit** (flesh only)
80g **Pineapple**
120g **Watermelon**
140ml **Coconut Water**
3 Ice Cubes

24g Carbs

2g Protein

1g Fat

2g Fibre

2 5-a-day

100 Cals

Nutrition Fact

Passion fruit is a rich source of vitamin C, helping to boost your body's immune system

Size
Medium
400g

Milkless Milkshake

Hard to believe this smooth, strawberry shake is completely dairy-free

Ingredients

16	Green Grapes
80g	Pineapple
4	Strawberries
80ml	Water
3	Ice Cubes

100 Cals

3 5-a-day

3g Fibre

0g Fat

1g Protein

25g Carbs

Size
Medium
360g

Recipe Tip
Try freezing your grapes for a super-cool smoothie

Sweet Potato Tang

A rare but balanced fusion of sour citrus and sweet potato

Ingredients

1/6	**Pink Grapefruit** (peeled)
1/3	**Orange** (peeled)
1/2	**Sweet Potato** (small, boiled)
120ml	Water
6	Ice Cubes

26g Carbs

2g Protein

0g Fat

5g Fibre

2½ 5-a-day

110 Cals

Nutrition Fact
Sweet potatoes are rich in fibre and a source of slow-releasing energy

Size
Medium
400g

Kiwi Yoshi

A crisp and delicate fruit & veg medley

Ingredients

1	**Kiwi** (peeled)
$1/8$	**Lime** (with skin)
$1/3$	**Mango**
$1/4$	**Red Apple**
60g	**Watermelon**
$1/8$	**Cucumber**
1	handful **Spinach**
80ml	Water
5	Ice Cubes

110 Cals

3½ 5-a-day

6g Fibre

1g Fat

2g Protein

25g Carbs

Size
Medium
425g

Recipe Tip
Add extra lime juice for a tangier taste

Pear Aplomb

The taste of autumn at any time of year

Ingredients

¼ **Pear** (cored)
2 **Plums** (destoned)
½ **Red Apple**
80ml Water
3 Ice Cubes

29g Carbs

2g Protein

0g Fat

7g Fibre

2½ 5-a-day

120 Cals

Nutrition Fact
Plums are rich in polyphenols which are
protective against heart disease

Size
Medium
420g

Rosie Rhubarb

A quirky mix of kiwi, rhubarb and rosemary to tickle your taste buds

Ingredients

½	**Green Apple**
1	**Kiwi** (peeled)
80g	**Rhubarb** (tinned)
1	sprig **Rosemary**
160ml	**Coconut Water**
3	Ice Cubes

120 Cals

2½ 5-a-day

4g Fibre

0g Fat

2g Protein

29g Carbs

Size
Medium
415g

Recipe Tip
If you don't have access to fresh rosemary,
leave it out or replace with another herb

Pick up a Pepper

This yellow pepper recipe makes for a savoury, off-beat blitz

Ingredients

½	**Pear** (cored)
¼	**Avocado** (no skin)
½	**Celery** stalk
2	handfuls **Spinach**
¼	**Yellow Pepper** (small)
¼	**Lime** (juice only)
140ml	Water
3	Ice Cubes

12g Carbs

3g Protein

7g Fat

7g Fibre

3 5-a-day

125 Cals

Nutrition Fact

Yellow peppers are high in beta-carotene, which helps avoid an itchy scalp and dry hair

Size
Medium
425g

Raspberry Ripple

This maple mingle is a marriage made in heaven

Ingredients

80g	Frozen Raspberries
1 tsp	Maple Syrup
160ml	Oat Milk

125 Cals

1 5-a-day

5g Fibre

3g Fat

2g Protein

21g Carbs

Size
Small
245g

Nutrition Fact
Oat milk is low in saturated fat and a
dairy-free alternative to cow's milk

Shady Spinach

An interesting, dusky mash-up

Ingredients

½	**Banana** (peeled)
40g	**Blueberries**
80g	**Watermelon**
⅛	**Cucumber**
2	handfuls **Spinach**
80ml	**Coconut Water**
3	Ice Cubes

28g Carbs

3g Protein

1g Fat

3g Fibre

3 5-a-day

125 Cals

Nutrition Fact
Elevate your mood by eating a
tryptophan-rich banana

Size

Medium
370g

Avofennel Fusion

A velvety mixture of fennel and avocado

Ingredients

80g	**Frozen Pineapple**
¼	**Avocado** (no skin)
40g	**Fennel**
½ tsp	**Chia Seeds**
½	**Lime** (juice only)
240ml	Water

125 Cals

2 5-a-day

5g Fibre

8g Fat

2g Protein

11g Carbs

Size
Medium
415g

Nutrition Fact
The selenium in fennel has been found to improve immune response to infection

Summer Zing

A sharp summer smoothie with half an orange and frozen fruit

Ingredients

80g	Frozen Summer Fruit
¼	Mango
½	Orange (peeled)
80g	Pineapple
100ml	Water

29g Carbs

3g Protein

1g Fat

8g Fibre

3½ 5-a-day

130 Cals

Nutrition Fact
Mango contains immune-boosting vitamin A

Size
Medium
420g

Kiwi Spotlight

A lively collection to keep you hydrated

Ingredients

40g	Blueberries
1	Kiwi (peeled)
1/3	Mango
80g	Watermelon
140ml	Coconut Water
3	Ice Cubes

135 Cals

3 5-a-day

4g Fibre

1g Fat

2g Protein

32g Carbs

Size
Medium
415g

Recipe Tip
If coconut water is not to your taste,
use water instead (and save 25 cals)

Almond Amore

This nutty papaya blend is earthy but balanced

Ingredients

½	**Banana** (peeled)
40g	**Blueberries**
½	**Papaya** (flesh only)
1	handful **Kale**
140ml	**Almond Milk**
3	Ice Cubes

30g Carbs

3g Protein

2g Fat

4g Fibre

2½ 5-a-day

145 Cals

Recipe Tip

To add 4g extra protein, replace almond with cow's milk (skimmed or semi-skimmed)

Size

Medium
410g

Choco Orange Date

A healthier alternative to chocolate orange pudding

Ingredients

1/6	**Orange**	(peeled)
4	**Dates**	(pitted)
1 tsp	**Cacao Powder**	
100ml	**Milk**	(semi-skimmed)
3	Ice Cubes	

150 Cals

1½ 5-a-day

3g Fibre

2g Fat

5g Protein

30g Carbs

Size
Small
215g

Nutrition Fact
Dates help to regulate heartbeat and blood pressure due to a high potassium content

Mandarin Cream

Thick, succulent, yogurty loveliness

Ingredients

1	**Banana** (small, peeled)
10	**Mandarin** segments
100g	**Soya Yogurt**
80ml	Water
3	Ice Cubes

27g Carbs
6g Protein
3g Fat
3g Fibre

2 5-a-day
150 Cals

Recipe Tip

No mandarins available? Use $1/3$ orange instead

Size
Medium
380g

Cream of Mango

A scrumptious mix with a hint of mint

Ingredients

80g	**Frozen Mango**
⅛	**Lime** (with skin)
80g	**Pineapple**
1 inch	**Ginger** (peeled)
5	**Mint** leaves
50g	**Greek Yogurt** (fat-free)
180ml	**Coconut Water**

150 Cals

2 5-a-day

4g Fibre

1g Fat

5g Protein

31g Carbs

Size
Medium
405g

Nutrition Fact
Ginger is known to alleviate discomfort and pain in the stomach

Choco Tropical

*Coconut Milk refers to the milk substitute, rather than tinned coconut milk (which is much more calorific!)

Double milk and chocolatey, but completely dairy-free

Ingredients

1	**Banana** (small, peeled)
80g	**Pineapple**
1 tsp	**Cacao Powder**
80ml	**Almond Milk**
80ml	**Coconut Milk***
5	**Ice Cubes**

34g Carbs

3g Protein

2g Fat

3g Fibre

2 5-a-day

155 Cals

Nutrition Fact

Coconut milk is lactose-free, so great for those who need to avoid dairy

Size
Medium
385g

Hello Yello

A sunny jumble of all things yellow to brighten up your day

Ingredients

2	**Apricots** (destoned)
1	**Banana** (small, peeled)
⅓	**Mango**
40g	**Pineapple**
1	**Yellow Plum** (destoned)
100ml	Water
3	Ice Cubes

160 Cals

3½ 5-a-day

6g Fibre

1g Fat

2g Protein

38g Carbs

Size
Medium
430g

Nutrition Fact
Pineapple helps with energy production in
the body due to its manganese content

Sweet Thyme

Elegantly balanced, with the novel addition of thyme

Ingredients

½	**Banana** (peeled)
½	**Green Apple**
⅙	**Orange** (peeled)
¼	**Pear** (cored)
1	sprig **Thyme**
1 tsp	**Honey**
80ml	**Almond Milk**
80ml	**Coconut Water**
3	**Ice Cubes**

39g Carbs

2g Protein

1g Fat

5g Fibre

2½ 5-a-day

165 Cals

Recipe Tip

If you like your smoothies less sweet, leave out the honey (and also save 15 cals)

Size
Medium
415g

Vanilla Date Shake

A short shot of heavenly chocolate pudding

Ingredients

½	**Banana** (peeled)
4	**Dates** (pitted)
½ tsp	**Chia Seeds**
1 tsp	**Cacao Powder**
Pinch	**Cinnamon**
Pinch	**Nutmeg**
2 drops	**Vanilla Essence**
140ml	**Hemp Milk**
3	Ice Cubes

170 Cals

1½ 5-a-day

4g Fibre

5g Fat

3g Protein

28g Carbs

Size
Small
270g

Nutrition Fact
Cacao is rich in flavonoids, antioxidants
that promote general good health

Cherry Afters

This simple recipe is full-flavoured thanks to the cherries and cacao

Ingredients

1	**Banana** (small, peeled)	
80g	**Frozen Cherries**	
1 tsp	**Cacao Powder**	
100ml	**Milk** (semi-skimmed)	

34g Carbs **6g** Protein **2g** Fat **3g** Fibre

2 5-a-day **175** Cals

Nutrition Fact

Milk is a great source of calcium for bone health, and B2 for healthy skin and eyes

Size
Small
265g

Toffee Apple

Tempt yourself with this sweet treat

Ingredients

1	**Green Apple** (small)
2	**Medjool Dates** (pitted)
Pinch	**Cinnamon**
½ tsp	**Rose Water**
180ml	Water
5	Ice Cubes

175 Cals

2 5-a-day

5g Fibre

0g Fat

1g Protein

43g Carbs

Size
Medium
415g

Recipe Tip
Can't get medjool dates? Use regular dates
(which have similar nutritional content)

Hannah Banana

An effortless ensemble that packs in the fruit

Ingredients

1	**Banana** (small, peeled)
60g	**Blueberries**
½	**Green Apple**
1	**Kiwi** (peeled)
100ml	Water
3	Ice Cubes

42g Carbs **2g** Protein **1g** Fat **6g** Fibre

3½ 5-a-day **180** Cals

Recipe Tip
For a thinner smoothie, only use ½ banana
(and also save 40 cals)

Size
Medium
415g

Figgin' Sweet

Satisfy your sweet tooth!

Ingredients

1	**Banana** (small, peeled)
¼	**Mango**
⅓	**Pear** (cored)
80g	**Watermelon**
1	**Dried Fig**
100ml	Water
3	Ice Cubes

180 Cals

3½ 5-a-day

6g Fibre

1g Fat

2g Protein

44g Carbs

Size
Medium
415g

Recipe Tip
For a cooler smoothie, replace fresh mango with frozen mango chunks

Cup o' Cacao

A curious combination of pistachio, watermelon and cacao

Ingredients

80g	Watermelon
1 tbsp	Raisins (heaped)
1 tbsp	Pistachio Kernels
2 tsp	Cacao Powder
Pinch	Cinnamon
100ml	Soya Milk
3	Ice Cubes

21g Carbs

7g Protein

9g Fat

3g Fibre

1½ 5-a-day

185 Cals

Recipe Tip
Leave out the pistachios to save 60 cals

Size
Small
250g

Seedy Satsuma

A ragbag recipe of spinach, seeds and satsuma

Ingredients

1/2 **Banana** (peeled)
80g **Pineapple**
1/4 **Red Apple**
1 **Satsuma** (peeled)
2 handfuls **Spinach**
1 tbsp **Mixed Seeds**
100ml Water
3 Ice Cubes

195 Cals

3½ 5-a-day

6g Fibre

6g Fat

5g Protein

33g Carbs

Size
Medium
440g

Recipe Tip
Omit the mixed seeds to save 60 cals

Peachy Hazels

You'll go nuts for this summery blend

Ingredients

10	**Cherries** (pitted)
1	**Peach** (destoned)
3	**Dried Apricots**
1 tbsp	**Hazelnuts**
120ml	**Almond Milk**
3	Ice Cubes

31g Carbs

5g Protein

8g Fat

6g Fibre

2½ 5-a-day

205 Cals

Nutrition Fact

Cherries are thought to raise melatonin levels and aid a good night's sleep

Size
Medium
405g

Almond Cheer

Banana, figs and chia seeds make this smoothie rich and creamy

Ingredients

½	**Banana** (small, peeled)
40g	**Blueberries**
4	**Strawberries**
2	**Dried Figs**
1 tsp	**Chia Seeds**
180ml	**Almond Milk**
3	**Ice Cubes**

215 Cals

3 5-a-day

7g Fibre

4g Fat

4g Protein

41g Carbs

Size
Medium
415g

Nutrition Fact
Chia seeds are high in fibre and an
excellent source of protein for vegans

Espresso Date

Put a spring in your step with this substitute for your morning latte

Ingredients

1	**Banana** (peeled)
4	**Dates** (pitted)
1 tbsp	**Almonds**
140ml	**Soya Milk**
60ml	**Espresso** (cooled)
3	Ice Cubes

37g Carbs

8g Protein

9g Fat

4g Fibre

2 5-a-day

255 Cals

Nutrition Fact
Almonds are heart-healthy due to their high vitamin E content

Size
Medium
380g

The Naughty Cup

Warning: This peanut butter shake is dangerously moreish!

Ingredients

1	**Banana** (small, peeled)
4	**Dates** (pitted)
1 tbsp	**Peanut Butter**
120ml	**Soya Milk**
2	Ice Cubes

255 Cals

2 5-a-day

4g Fibre

10g Fat

9g Protein

33g Carbs

Size
Small
265g

Nutrition Fact
Soya milk is rich in isoflavones and soluble fibre, which keep your heart healthy

Lettuce Be

An unconventional mingle of banana, lettuce and sweet potato

Ingredients

½	**Banana** (peeled)
2 tbsp	**Raisins** (heaped)
40g	**Lettuce**
½	**Sweet Potato** (small, boiled)
1 tbsp	**Cashews**
Pinch	**Cinnamon**
140ml	**Almond Milk**
6	Ice Cubes

56g Carbs
5g Protein
7g Fat
6g Fibre

3 5-a-day
295 Cals

Nutrition Fact

Cashew nuts are a good source of zinc, essential for enhancing your memory

Size

Medium
430g

Melon Salad

Get 5 of your 5-a-day for just 90 cals!

Ingredients

60g	Galia Melon
40g	Asparagus tips
1	Broccoli floret
1	Cauliflower floret
½	Carrot
½	Celery stalk
⅙	Courgette
⅛	Cucumber
40g	Lettuce
10	Mint leaves
½	Lemon (juice only)
100ml	Water
5	Ice Cubes

90 Cals

5 5-a-day

7g Fibre

2g Fat

7g Protein

12g Carbs

Size
Large
575g

Nutrition Fact
Broccoli is high in vitamin K, which
is needed for wound healing

Chris's Cauli

A surprisingly tasty mix of cauliflower and apple with a hint of aniseed!

Ingredients

½	Red Apple
2	Cauliflower florets
1	Carrot
¼	Cucumber
80g	Fennel
2 inch	Ginger (peeled)
½	Lime (juice only)
140ml	Water
6	Ice Cubes

21g Carbs   **4g** Protein   **1g** Fat   **9g** Fibre

5 5-a-day   **110** Cals

Nutrition Fact

Sulforaphane in cauliflower has been found to improve blood pressure and kidney function

Size
Large
630g

Melon Mayhem!

Four types of melon in this bouncy blend

Ingredients

80g	Cantaloupe Melon
80g	Galia Melon
80g	Honeydew Melon
1/6	Orange (peeled)
4	Strawberries
80g	Watermelon
1 inch	Ginger (peeled)
50ml	Water
5	Ice Cubes

120 Cals

5½ 5-a-day

4g Fibre

1g Fat

3g Protein

27g Carbs

Size
Large
555g

Recipe Tip
Add extra ginger if you want a stronger punch to your smoothie experience!

Multi Mix-up

An assortment of wholesome goodness

Ingredients

40g	Blueberries
8	Green Grapes
¼	Lime (with skin)
¼	Pear (cored)
40g	Pineapple
½	Plum (destoned)
4	Raspberries
2	Strawberries
½	Carrot
½	Celery stalk
⅛	Cucumber
80ml	Water
5	Ice Cubes

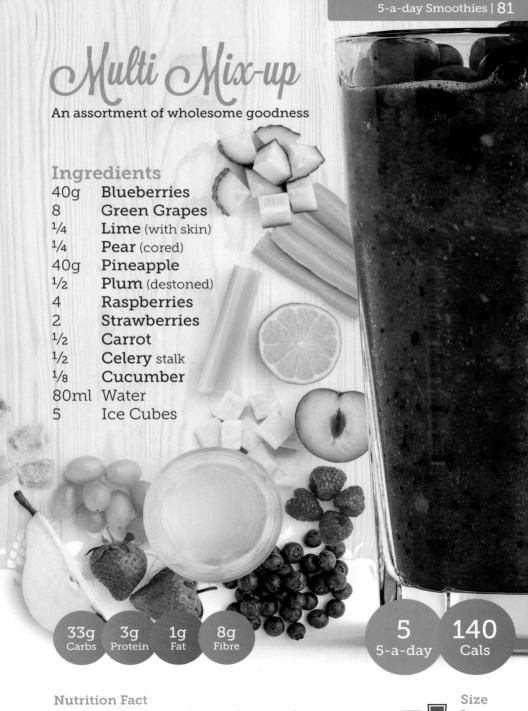

33g Carbs

3g Protein

1g Fat

8g Fibre

5 5-a-day

140 Cals

Nutrition Fact
Cucumbers contain fisetin that may have
an important role in brain health

Size
Large
545g

Burgundy Zinger

Give yourself a high-5 with this earthy mix

Ingredients

1/8	**Lemon**	(with skin)
1/3	**Orange**	(peeled)
1/4	**Pear**	(cored)
80g	**Pineapple**	
1 1/2	**Boiled Beetroot**	(small)
1/2	**Carrot**	
40g	**Red Cabbage**	
2	handfuls **Spinach**	
100ml	Water	
3	Ice Cubes	

145 Cals

5 5-a-day

10g Fibre

1g Fat

5g Protein

31g Carbs

Size
Large
540g

Nutrition Fact
Red cabbage is high in vitamin K for maintaining bone strength and health

Kiwi Kicker

Getting all 5 of your 5-a-day fruit & veg
has never been easier!

Ingredients

1	**Apricot** (destoned)
½	**Banana** (peeled)
80g	**Honeydew Melon**
1	**Kiwi** (peeled)
10	**Mandarin** segments
80g	**Pineapple**
2	handfuls **Spinach**
100ml	Water
5	Ice Cubes

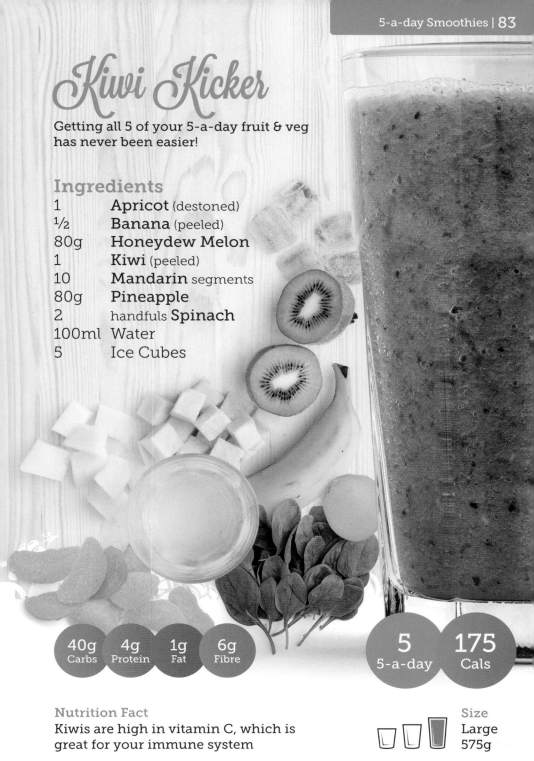

40g Carbs

4g Protein

1g Fat

6g Fibre

5 5-a-day

175 Cals

Nutrition Fact
Kiwis are high in vitamin C, which is
great for your immune system

Size
Large
575g

Strawberry Barb

5 of your 5-a-day with just 5 ingredients!

Ingredients

6	Lychees
½	Mango
½	Red Apple
4	Strawberries
80g	**Rhubarb** (tinned)
120ml	Water
6	Ice Cubes

175 Cals

5 5-a-day

8g Fibre

0g Fat

3g Protein

43g Carbs

Size
Large
600g

Recipe Tip
If in season, try using fresh rhubarb
(but make sure you stew it first)

Bittersweet Rose

Rich and fruity with a zesty aftertaste

Ingredients

80g	**Frozen Mango**
10	**Mandarin** segments
⅙	**Orange** (peeled)
80g	**Pineapple**
⅙	**Red Grapefruit** (peeled)
4	**Strawberries**
1 tsp	**Rose Water**
120ml	**Coconut Water**

42g Carbs **3g** Protein **1g** Fat **7g** Fibre

5 5-a-day **180** Cals

Recipe Tip
For a less sour taste, leave out the grapefruit

Size
Large
525g

Great Greens

Big green glass of savoury wholesomeness!

Ingredients

80g	Frozen Pineapple
½	Green Apple
¼	Avocado (no skin)
1	Broccoli floret
⅓	Courgette
2	handfuls Kale
2	handfuls Spinach
2	sprigs Parsley
1 tsp	Wheatgrass Powder
230ml	Water

205 Cals

5 5-a-day

11g Fibre

9g Fat

8g Protein

24g Carbs

Size
Large
630g

Nutrition Fact
Avocados are high in omega 3, which may
play a role in preventing dementia

Sweet Beet

Double dried fruit in this thick smoothie
helps to pack in 6 of your 5-a-day!

Ingredients

80g	Frozen Blueberries
⅙	Orange (peeled)
80g	Pineapple
2	Dried Apple Rings
2 tbsp	Raisins (heaped)
½	Carrot
1	Raw Beetroot (peeled)
40g	Red Cabbage
200ml	Water

| 60g Carbs | 4g Protein | 1g Fat | 11g Fibre | | 6 5-a-day | 255 Cals |

Recipe Tip

Leave out the raisins to save 21g carbs
and 80 cals (making it 5 of your 5-a-day)

Size
Large
605g

Fruit Pod

A delicious way to get a whopping 10g fibre

Ingredients

8	Blackberries
1/3	Mango
1/6	Orange (peeled)
1/2	Peach (destoned)
8	Raspberries
5	Red Grapes
1/4	Vanilla Pod (seeds only)
80ml	Water
3	Ice Cubes

130 Cals

4 5-a-day

10g Fibre

1g Fat

3g Protein

30g Carbs

Size
Medium
450g

Recipe Tip
Use 1 or 2 drops of vanilla essence if
you don't have a vanilla pod available

Passion for Prunes

This revitalising fusion is earthy and thirst-quenching

Ingredients

80g	**Frozen Blueberries**
½	**Passion Fruit** (flesh only)
4	**Raspberries**
4	**Prunes** (small, destoned)
1 inch	**Ginger** (peeled)
2	handfuls **Kale**
1 tsp	**Chia Seeds**
100ml	**Green Tea** (cooled)
120ml	Water

22g Carbs

5g Protein

3g Fat

9g Fibre

3 5-a-day

130 Cals

Nutrition Fact
Antioxidant catechin and caffeine in green tea may help the body burn more calories

Size
Medium
420g

Parsnip Badger

Parsnips provide a quirky way to add extra fibre to your smoothie

Ingredients

½	**Banana** (peeled)
80g	**Pineapple**
1	**Carrot**
1	**Parsnip** (boiled)
120ml	Water
6	Ice Cubes

160 Cals

3½ 5-a-day

10g Fibre

2g Fat

3g Protein

36g Carbs

Size
Medium
490g

Nutrition Fact
Parsnips are a good source of iron, which
is important in preventing anaemia

Satin Berry Smooth

A glass of velvety lusciousness, sweetened with figs

Ingredients

8	Blackberries
16	Raspberries
2	Dried Figs
100g	Natural Yogurt (fat-free)
80ml	Water
3	Ice Cubes

31g Carbs   **9g** Protein   **1g** Fat   **9g** Fibre

3 5-a-day   **160** Cals

Nutrition Fact

Natural yogurt contains probiotics, which support a healthy digestive system

Size
Medium
410g

Grass in a Glass

Like the smell of freshly-cut grass on a spring morning
(but in a thick, creamy smoothie!)

Ingredients

½	**Pear** (cored)
1	**Red Apple** (small)
¼	**Avocado** (no skin)
2	handfuls **Kale**
1	sprig **Parsley** (large)
¼	**Lime** (juice only)
140ml	Water
3	Ice Cubes

175 Cals

3 5-a-day

9g Fibre

8g Fat

3g Protein

25g Carbs

Size
Medium
480g

Recipe Tip
Replace the parsley with any other
fresh herb of your liking

Double Coconut

This radiant smoothie tastes as good as it looks

Ingredients

2	**Apricots** (destoned)
20g	**Coconut**
½	**Mango**
1	**Raw Beetroot** (peeled)
160ml	**Coconut Water**
3	Ice Cubes

29g Carbs

3g Protein

8g Fat

8g Fibre

3 5-a-day

190 Cals

Recipe Tip

If raw beetroot is not available, use cooked beetroot (not in vinegar!)

Size
Medium
440g

Berry Velvety

This banana berry blend is a yummy way
to get 8g fibre and 4 of your 5-a-day

Ingredients

1	**Banana** (small, peeled)
16	**Raspberries**
4	**Strawberries**
4	**Prunes** (small, destoned)
100ml	**Soya Milk**
5	Ice Cubes

210 Cals

4 5-a-day

8g Fibre

3g Fat

7g Protein

41g Carbs

Size
Medium
430g

Nutrition Fact
Prunes are high in soluble fibre, which
helps to lower cholesterol levels

The Apricotty

Hemp powder and dried apricots provide a powerful punch

*Coconut Milk refers to the milk substitute, rather than tinned coconut milk (which is much more calorific!)

Ingredients

½	Mango
80g	Pineapple
6	Dried Apricots
1 tbsp	Hemp Protein Powder
2 drops	Vanilla Essence
140ml	Coconut Milk*
6	Ice Cubes

41g Carbs

8g Protein

2g Fat

9g Fibre

3 5-a-day

210 Cals

Nutrition Fact

Dried apricots are a great non-dairy source of calcium needed for bone and dental health

Size
Medium
425g

Ready Racer

Get yourself moving with this breakfast replacement

Ingredients

½	Banana (peeled)
80g	Blueberries
2 tbsp	Pomegranate Seeds
2 tbsp	Oat Bran
1 tsp	Honey
140ml	Oat Milk
5	Ice Cubes

280 Cals

2 5-a-day

8g Fibre

4g Fat

6g Protein

52g Carbs

Size
Medium
385g

Recipe Tip
You can substitute oat bran for
another high-fibre cereal

Muesli in the Morning

Muesli is a source of slow-releasing energy in this rich, substantial smoothie

Ingredients

20g	Coconut
12	Raspberries
1 tbsp	Raisins (heaped)
4 tbsp	Muesli
200ml	Almond Milk
6	Ice Cubes

40g Carbs

6g Protein

12g Fat

8g Fibre

1½ 5-a-day

285 Cals

Recipe Tip

Reduce the muesli to 2 tbsp to save 55 cals (this will reduce the fibre by 1g)

Size

Medium
405g

Pomegranate Greek

A yogurty marriage of berries and pomegranate seeds

Ingredients

80g	Blueberries
80g	Frozen Raspberries
2 tbsp	Pomegranate Seeds (heaped)
100g	Greek Yogurt (fat-free)
100ml	Water

180 Cals

2½ 5-a-day

7g Fibre

1g Fat

10g Protein

28g Carbs

Size
Medium
400g

Recipe Tip
For a dairy-free smoothie, use soya yogurt in place of Greek yogurt

Planting a Seed

Luscious and flavoursome with black forest fruit

Ingredients

80g	**Frozen Black Forest Fruit**
1	**Kiwi** (peeled)
3	**Strawberries**
1 tbsp	**Mixed Seeds**
100g	**Natural Yogurt** (fat-free)
100ml	Water

25g Carbs

10g Protein

6g Fat

5g Fibre

2½ 5-a-day

195 Cals

Recipe Tip
If black forest fruit is not available, you can use other frozen berries

Size
Medium
405g

Oaty Cinny

Suitable as a breakfast replacement
or a yogurty pudding

Ingredients

8	Blackberries
40g	Frozen Blueberries
½	Red Apple
3 tbsp	Oats
Pinch	Cinnamon
100g	**Natural Yogurt** (fat-free)
100ml	**Milk** (semi-skimmed)

235 Cals

2½ 5-a-day

8g Fibre

3g Fat

12g Protein

39g Carbs

Size
Medium
415g

Recipe Tip
Switching to skimmed milk will save 2g fat
and 15 cals (but will not affect the protein)

Beetroot Brekkie

This oddball combination of beetroot and muesli is surprisingly scrumptious!

Ingredients

80g	**Frozen Summer Fruit**
1/3	**Orange** (peeled)
2	**Boiled Beetroot** (small)
4 tbsp	**Muesli**
100g	**Natural Yogurt** (fat-free)
80ml	Water

47g Carbs

12g Protein

3g Fat

9g Fibre

3 5-a-day

260 Cals

Recipe Tip

Use an organic fruit yogurt for an alternative taste

Size
Medium
450g

Nuts & Whey

Use of whey protein powder makes this
our highest-protein smoothie

Ingredients

1	**Banana** (small, peeled)
4	**Strawberries**
2	handfuls **Kale**
1 tsp	**Cacao Powder**
2 tbsp	**Whey Protein Powder**
2 tsp	**Peanut Butter**
140ml	**Coconut Water**
3	**Ice Cubes**

260 Cals

2½ 5-a-day

6g Fibre

7g Fat

17g Protein

34g Carbs

Size
Large
410g

Recipe Tip
Allergic to peanuts? Try a different nut
butter such as almond or cashew

Hempy Vegan

A thick, salubrious and wholesome shake

Ingredients

½	**Banana** (peeled)
60g	**Blueberries**
8	**Raspberries**
2	**Dates** (pitted)
¼	**Avocado** (no skin)
1 tbsp	**Hemp Protein Powder**
120ml	**Soya Milk**
120ml	Water
6	Ice Cubes

37g Carbs   **11g** Protein   **11g** Fat   **8g** Fibre

2½ 5-a-day   **295** Cals

Recipe Tip
If hemp isn't your thing, replace it with whey protein powder (which is non-vegan)

Size
Large
530g

Protein Powershake

A quick and easy way to get 15g protein

Ingredients

1	**Banana** (small, peeled)
20g	**Coconut**
2	**Dried Figs**
2 tbsp	**Whey Protein Powder**
180ml	**Almond Milk**
3	Ice Cubes

315 Cals

2 5-a-day

7g Fibre

11g Fat

15g Protein

42g Carbs

Size
Medium
365g

Nutrition Fact
Figs contain prebiotics to promote
a healthy digestive system

Carbs & Cals Waldorf

Our glorious spin on the famous salad... but in a glass

Ingredients

½	**Green Apple**
1 tbsp	**Sultanas** (heaped)
2 tbsp	**Walnuts**
1 tsp	**Maple Syrup**
100g	**Natural Yogurt** (fat-free)
140ml	**Milk** (semi-skimmed)
3	Ice Cubes

38g Carbs

14g Protein

16g Fat

3g Fibre

1½ 5-a-day

350 Cals

Nutrition Fact

Walnuts are anti-inflammatory, so great for those suffering with joint pain and arthritis

Size
Medium
400g

Morning Glory

A perfect high-protein breakfast replacement, packing 17g per glass

Ingredients

½	Banana (peeled)
80g	Frozen Summer Fruit
8	Green Grapes
¼	Mango
½	Carrot
⅛	Cucumber
2	handfuls Spinach
4 tbsp	Muesli
1 tbsp	Pumpkin Seeds
100g	Greek Yogurt (fat-free)
120ml	Water

375 Cals

4 5-a-day

12g Fibre

8g Fat

17g Protein

59g Carbs

Size
Large
590g

Nutrition Fact
Pumpkin seeds help keep your skin healthy, thanks to their rich iodine content

Peanut Butter Cup

Intense cup of banana and peanut butter loveliness; a real treat!

Ingredients
½   **Banana** (peeled)
1 tbsp   **Dried Cranberries** (heaped)
4 tbsp   **Oats**
1 tbsp   **Sunflower Seeds**
1 tbsp   **Peanut Butter**
120ml   **Oat Milk**
3   Ice Cubes

49g Carbs **10g** Protein **16g** Fat **6g** Fibre

1 5-a-day **375** Cals

Nutrition Fact
Sunflower seeds are high in magnesium, which is linked to protecting against type 2 diabetes

Size
Small
270g

Muesli
15g, 2 tbsp

2g Protein
1g Fat
2g Fibre
10g Carbs
55 Cals
0 5-a-day

Muesli
30g, 4 tbsp

3g Protein
2g Fat
3g Fibre
20g Carbs
110 Cals
0 5-a-day

Oat Bran
10g, 1 tbsp

1g Protein
1g Fat
2g Fibre
5g Carbs
36 Cals
0 5-a-day

Oat Bran
20g, 2 tbsp

3g Protein
2g Fat
4g Fibre
9g Carbs
73 Cals
0 5-a-day

Oats
10g, 2 tbsp

1g Protein
1g Fat
1g Fibre
6g Carbs
37 Cals
0 5-a-day

Oats
20g, 4 tbsp

2g Protein
1g Fat
2g Fibre
12g Carbs
74 Cals
0 5-a-day

Apple Rings
15g

0g Protein
0g Fat
2g Fibre
9g Carbs
36 Cals
½ 5-a-day

Apple Rings
30g

1g Protein
0g Fat
4g Fibre
18g Carbs
71 Cals
1 5-a-day

Apricots
15g

1g Protein
0g Fat
2g Fibre
7g Carbs
28 Cals
½ 5-a-day

Apricots
30g

1g Protein
0g Fat
3g Fibre
13g Carbs
56 Cals
1 5-a-day

Cranberries
15g, 1 heaped tbsp

0g Protein
0g Fat
1g Fibre
12g Carbs
51 Cals
½ 5-a-day

Cranberries
30g, 2 heaped tbsp

0g Protein
0g Fat
1g Fibre
24g Carbs
102 Cals
1 5-a-day

Dates
15g

- 0g Protein
- 0g Fat
- 1g Fibre
- 10g Carbs
- 41 Cals
- ½ 5-a-day

Dates
30g

- 1g Protein
- 0g Fat
- 2g Fibre
- 20g Carbs
- 81 Cals
- 1 5-a-day

Figs
15g

- 1g Protein
- 0g Fat
- 2g Fibre
- 8g Carbs
- 34 Cals
- ½ 5-a-day

Figs
30g

- 1g Protein
- 0g Fat
- 3g Fibre
- 16g Carbs
- 68 Cals
- 1 5-a-day

Goji Berries
3g, 1 tsp

- 0g Protein
- 0g Fat
- 0g Fibre
- 2g Carbs
- 10 Cals
- 0 5-a-day

Goji Berries
8g, 1 tbsp

- 1g Protein
- 0g Fat
- 1g Fibre
- 5g Carbs
- 26 Cals
- 0 5-a-day

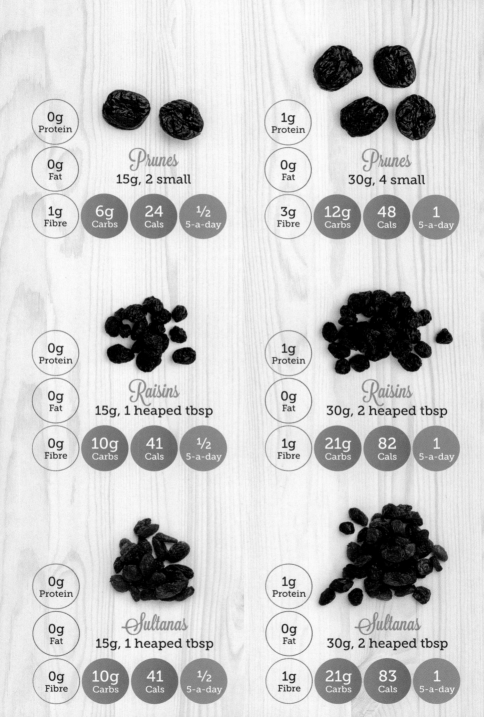

Prunes
15g, 2 small

- 0g Protein
- 0g Fat
- 1g Fibre
- 6g Carbs
- 24 Cals
- ½ 5-a-day

Prunes
30g, 4 small

- 1g Protein
- 0g Fat
- 3g Fibre
- 12g Carbs
- 48 Cals
- 1 5-a-day

Raisins
15g, 1 heaped tbsp

- 0g Protein
- 0g Fat
- 0g Fibre
- 10g Carbs
- 41 Cals
- ½ 5-a-day

Raisins
30g, 2 heaped tbsp

- 1g Protein
- 0g Fat
- 1g Fibre
- 21g Carbs
- 82 Cals
- 1 5-a-day

Sultanas
15g, 1 heaped tbsp

- 0g Protein
- 0g Fat
- 0g Fibre
- 10g Carbs
- 41 Cals
- ½ 5-a-day

Sultanas
30g, 2 heaped tbsp

- 1g Protein
- 0g Fat
- 1g Fibre
- 21g Carbs
- 83 Cals
- 1 5-a-day

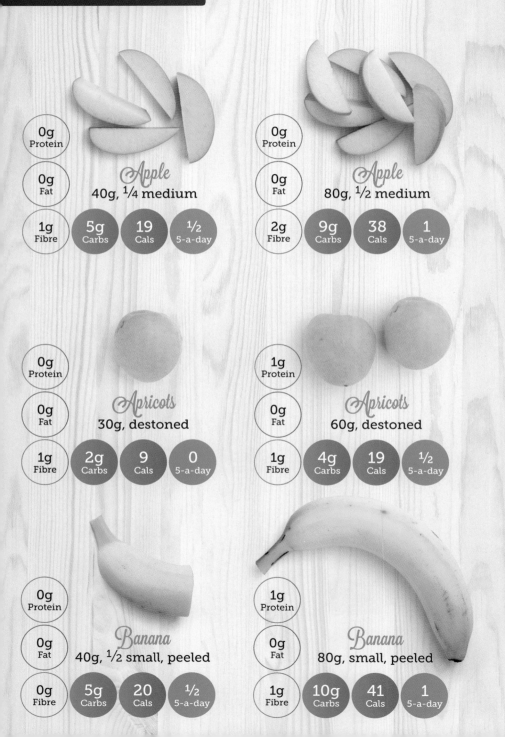

Apple
40g, ¼ medium

- 0g Protein
- 0g Fat
- 1g Fibre
- 5g Carbs
- 19 Cals
- ½ 5-a-day

Apple
80g, ½ medium

- 0g Protein
- 0g Fat
- 2g Fibre
- 9g Carbs
- 38 Cals
- 1 5-a-day

Apricots
30g, destoned

- 0g Protein
- 0g Fat
- 1g Fibre
- 2g Carbs
- 9 Cals
- 0 5-a-day

Apricots
60g, destoned

- 1g Protein
- 0g Fat
- 1g Fibre
- 4g Carbs
- 19 Cals
- ½ 5-a-day

Banana
40g, ½ small, peeled

- 0g Protein
- 0g Fat
- 0g Fibre
- 5g Carbs
- 20 Cals
- ½ 5-a-day

Banana
80g, small, peeled

- 1g Protein
- 0g Fat
- 1g Fibre
- 10g Carbs
- 41 Cals
- 1 5-a-day

Blackberries
40g

- 0g Protein
- 0g Fat
- 2g Fibre
- 2g Carbs
- 10 Cals
- ½ 5-a-day

Blackberries
80g

- 1g Protein
- 0g Fat
- 3g Fibre
- 4g Carbs
- 20 Cals
- 1 5-a-day

Blueberries
40g

- 0g Protein
- 0g Fat
- 1g Fibre
- 6g Carbs
- 26 Cals
- ½ 5-a-day

Blueberries
80g

- 1g Protein
- 0g Fat
- 2g Fibre
- 11g Carbs
- 53 Cals
- 1 5-a-day

Cantaloupe
40g

- 0g Protein
- 0g Fat
- 1g Fibre
- 2g Carbs
- 8 Cals
- ½ 5-a-day

Cantaloupe
80g

- 0g Protein
- 0g Fat
- 1g Fibre
- 3g Carbs
- 15 Cals
- 1 5-a-day

0g Protein			
0g Fat			
0g Fibre	5g Carbs	19 Cals	½ 5-a-day

Cherries
40g, destoned

1g Protein			
0g Fat			
1g Fibre	9g Carbs	38 Cals	1 5-a-day

Cherries
80g, destoned

1g Protein			
7g Fat			
2g Fibre	1g Carbs	70 Cals	0 5-a-day

Coconut
20g

1g Protein			
14g Fat			
4g Fibre	1g Carbs	140 Cals	½ 5-a-day

Coconut
40g

0g Protein			
0g Fat			
1g Fibre	3g Carbs	13 Cals	0 5-a-day

Figs
30g

1g Protein			
0g Fat			
1g Fibre	6g Carbs	26 Cals	½ 5-a-day

Figs
60g

Galia Melon
40g

- 0g Protein
- 0g Fat
- 0g Fibre
- 2g Carbs
- 10 Cals
- ½ 5-a-day

Galia Melon
80g

- 0g Protein
- 0g Fat
- 0g Fibre
- 4g Carbs
- 19 Cals
- 1 5-a-day

Grapefruit
40g, ⅙ medium, peeled

- 0g Protein
- 0g Fat
- 1g Fibre
- 3g Carbs
- 12 Cals
- ½ 5-a-day

Grapefruit
80g, ⅓ medium, peeled

- 1g Protein
- 0g Fat
- 1g Fibre
- 5g Carbs
- 24 Cals
- 1 5-a-day

Grapes
40g

- 0g Protein
- 0g Fat
- 0g Fibre
- 6g Carbs
- 24 Cals
- ½ 5-a-day

Grapes
80g

- 0g Protein
- 0g Fat
- 1g Fibre
- 12g Carbs
- 48 Cals
- 1 5-a-day

Honeydew Melon
40g

0g Protein			
0g Fat			
0g Fibre	3g Carbs	11 Cals	½ 5-a-day

Honeydew Melon
80g

0g Protein			
0g Fat			
1g Fibre	5g Carbs	22 Cals	1 5-a-day

Kiwi
55g, peeled

1g Protein			
0g Fat			
1g Fibre	6g Carbs	27 Cals	½ 5-a-day

Kiwi
110g, peeled

1g Protein			
1g Fat			
3g Fibre	12g Carbs	54 Cals	1 5-a-day

Lemon
15g, ⅛ with skin

0g Protein			
0g Fat			
0g Fibre	0g Carbs	3 Cals	0 5-a-day

Lemon
30g, ¼ with skin

0g Protein			
0g Fat			
0g Fibre	1g Carbs	6 Cals	0 5-a-day

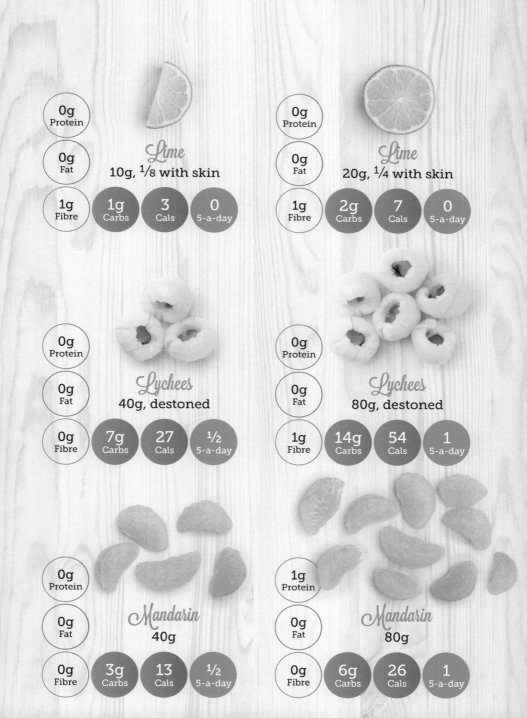

0g Protein
0g Fat
1g Fibre

Lime
10g, ⅛ with skin

1g Carbs | 3 Cals | 0 5-a-day

0g Protein
0g Fat
1g Fibre

Lime
20g, ¼ with skin

2g Carbs | 7 Cals | 0 5-a-day

0g Protein
0g Fat
0g Fibre

Lychees
40g, destoned

7g Carbs | 27 Cals | ½ 5-a-day

0g Protein
0g Fat
1g Fibre

Lychees
80g, destoned

14g Carbs | 54 Cals | 1 5-a-day

0g Protein
0g Fat
0g Fibre

Mandarin
40g

3g Carbs | 13 Cals | ½ 5-a-day

1g Protein
0g Fat
0g Fibre

Mandarin
80g

6g Carbs | 26 Cals | 1 5-a-day

Mango
40g, ¼ medium

0g Protein
0g Fat
1g Fibre
6g Carbs
23 Cals
½ 5-a-day

Mango
80g, ½ medium

1g Protein
0g Fat
3g Fibre
11g Carbs
46 Cals
1 5-a-day

Nectarine
60g, destoned

1g Protein
0g Fat
1g Fibre
5g Carbs
24 Cals
½ 5-a-day

Nectarine
120g, destoned

2g Protein
0g Fat
2g Fibre
11g Carbs
48 Cals
1 5-a-day

Orange
40g, ⅙ medium, peeled

0g Protein
0g Fat
1g Fibre
3g Carbs
15 Cals
½ 5-a-day

Orange
80g, ⅓ medium, peeled

1g Protein
0g Fat
2g Fibre
7g Carbs
30 Cals
1 5-a-day

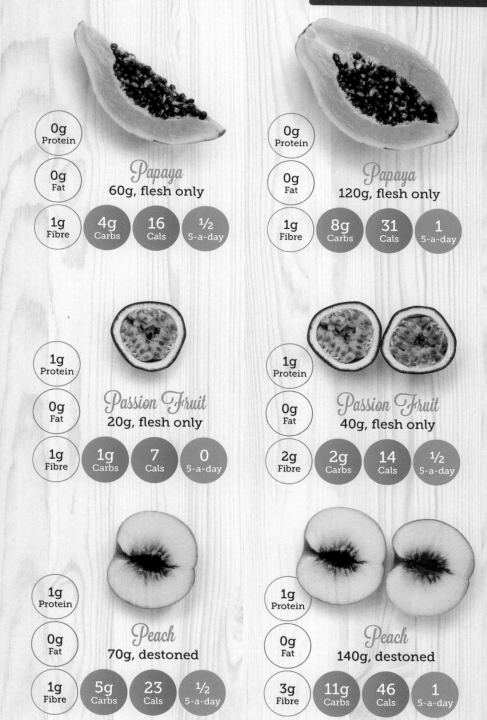

0g Protein

0g Fat

1g Fibre

Papaya
60g, flesh only

4g Carbs | **16** Cals | **½** 5-a-day

0g Protein

0g Fat

1g Fibre

Papaya
120g, flesh only

8g Carbs | **31** Cals | **1** 5-a-day

1g Protein

0g Fat

1g Fibre

Passion Fruit
20g, flesh only

1g Carbs | **7** Cals | **0** 5-a-day

1g Protein

0g Fat

2g Fibre

Passion Fruit
40g, flesh only

2g Carbs | **14** Cals | **½** 5-a-day

1g Protein

0g Fat

1g Fibre

Peach
70g, destoned

5g Carbs | **23** Cals | **½** 5-a-day

1g Protein

0g Fat

3g Fibre

Peach
140g, destoned

11g Carbs | **46** Cals | **1** 5-a-day

Pear
40g, cored

0g Protein
0g Fat
1g Fibre
4g Carbs
16 Cals
½ 5-a-day

Pear
80g, cored

0g Protein
0g Fat
2g Fibre
8g Carbs
32 Cals
1 5-a-day

Persimmon
70g

1g Protein
0g Fat
1g Fibre
14g Carbs
58 Cals
½ 5-a-day

Persimmon
140g

1g Protein
0g Fat
2g Fibre
27g Carbs
116 Cals
1 5-a-day

Pineapple
40g

0g Protein
0g Fat
1g Fibre
4g Carbs
16 Cals
½ 5-a-day

Pineapple
80g

0g Protein
0g Fat
1g Fibre
8g Carbs
33 Cals
1 5-a-day

0g
Protein

0g
Fat

1g
Fibre

Plum
45g, destoned

4g
Carbs

16
Cals

½
5-a-day

1g
Protein

0g
Fat

2g
Fibre

Plum
90g, destoned

8g
Carbs

32
Cals

1
5-a-day

0g
Protein

0g
Fat

1g
Fibre

Pomegranate Seeds
20g, 1 heaped tbsp

3g
Carbs

17
Cals

0
5-a-day

1g
Protein

0g
Fat

1g
Fibre

Pomegranate Seeds
40g, 2 heaped tbsp

6g
Carbs

34
Cals

½
5-a-day

1g
Protein

0g
Fat

1g
Fibre

Raspberries
40g

2g
Carbs

10
Cals

½
5-a-day

1g
Protein

0g
Fat

3g
Fibre

Raspberries
80g

4g
Carbs

20
Cals

1
5-a-day

Satsuma
40g, peeled

0g Protein
0g Fat
1g Fibre
3g Carbs
14 Cals
½ 5-a-day

Satsuma
80g, peeled

1g Protein
0g Fat
1g Fibre
7g Carbs
29 Cals
1 5-a-day

Strawberries
40g

0g Protein
0g Fat
1g Fibre
2g Carbs
11 Cals
½ 5-a-day

Strawberries
80g

1g Protein
0g Fat
1g Fibre
5g Carbs
22 Cals
1 5-a-day

Watermelon
40g

0g Protein
0g Fat
0g Fibre
3g Carbs
12 Cals
½ 5-a-day

Watermelon
80g

0g Protein
0g Fat
0g Fibre
6g Carbs
25 Cals
1 5-a-day

0g Protein			
0g Fat	**Frozen Blueberries** 40g		
1g Fibre	4g Carbs	19 Cals	½ 5-a-day

1g Protein			
0g Fat	**Frozen Blueberries** 80g		
2g Fibre	8g Carbs	38 Cals	1 5-a-day

0g Protein			
0g Fat	**Frozen Cherries** 40g		
0g Fibre	5g Carbs	21 Cals	½ 5-a-day

1g Protein			
0g Fat	**Frozen Cherries** 80g		
1g Fibre	9g Carbs	42 Cals	1 5-a-day

0g Protein			
0g Fat	**Frozen Mango** 40g		
1g Fibre	6g Carbs	27 Cals	½ 5-a-day

1g Protein			
0g Fat	**Frozen Mango** 80g		
2g Fibre	11g Carbs	54 Cals	1 5-a-day

0g Protein
0g Fat
1g Fibre

Frozen Mixed Berries
40g

2g Carbs
15 Cals
½ 5-a-day

1g Protein
0g Fat
3g Fibre

Frozen Mixed Berries
80g

5g Carbs
29 Cals
1 5-a-day

0g Protein
0g Fat
1g Fibre

Frozen Pineapple
40g

5g Carbs
22 Cals
½ 5-a-day

0g Protein
0g Fat
1g Fibre

Frozen Pineapple
80g

10g Carbs
44 Cals
1 5-a-day

1g Protein
0g Fat
2g Fibre

Frozen Raspberries
40g

3g Carbs
19 Cals
½ 5-a-day

1g Protein
0g Fat
4g Fibre

Frozen Raspberries
80g

6g Carbs
37 Cals
1 5-a-day

0g Protein

0g Fat

0g Fibre

Basil
6 leaves

0g Carbs

1 Cals

0 5-a-day

0g Protein

0g Fat

0g Fibre

Coriander
large sprig

0g Carbs

1 Cals

0 5-a-day

0g Protein

0g Fat

0g Fibre

Mint
5 leaves

0g Carbs

1 Cals

0 5-a-day

0g Protein

0g Fat

0g Fibre

Parsley
large sprig

0g Carbs

1 Cals

0 5-a-day

0g Protein

0g Fat

0g Fibre

Rosemary
sprig

0g Carbs

1 Cals

0 5-a-day

0g Protein

0g Fat

0g Fibre

Thyme
sprig

0g Carbs

1 Cals

0 5-a-day

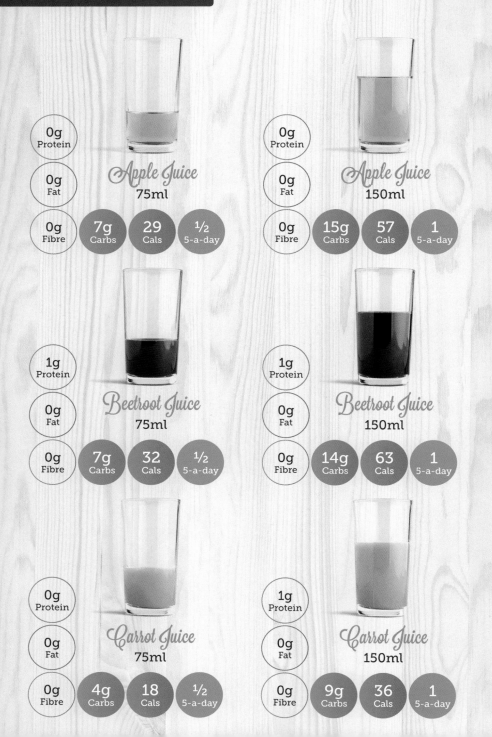

Apple Juice
75ml

0g Protein
0g Fat
0g Fibre
7g Carbs
29 Cals
½ 5-a-day

Apple Juice
150ml

0g Protein
0g Fat
0g Fibre
15g Carbs
57 Cals
1 5-a-day

Beetroot Juice
75ml

1g Protein
0g Fat
0g Fibre
7g Carbs
32 Cals
½ 5-a-day

Beetroot Juice
150ml

1g Protein
0g Fat
0g Fibre
14g Carbs
63 Cals
1 5-a-day

Carrot Juice
75ml

0g Protein
0g Fat
0g Fibre
4g Carbs
18 Cals
½ 5-a-day

Carrot Juice
150ml

1g Protein
0g Fat
0g Fibre
9g Carbs
36 Cals
1 5-a-day

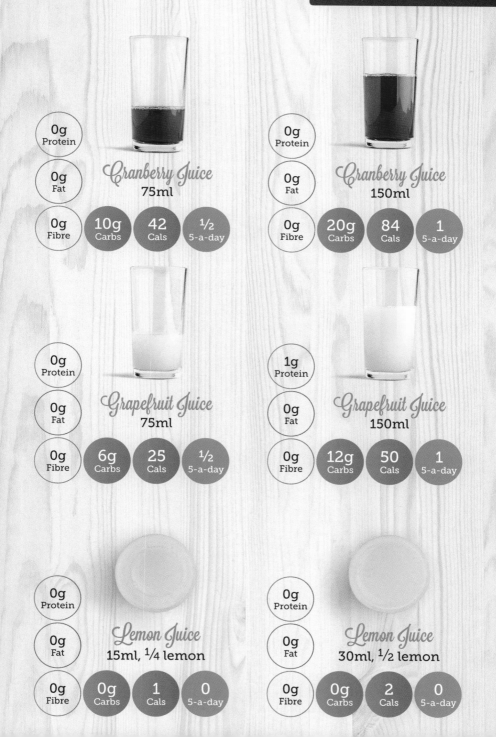

Cranberry Juice
75ml

0g Protein
0g Fat
0g Fibre
10g Carbs
42 Cals
½ 5-a-day

Cranberry Juice
150ml

0g Protein
0g Fat
0g Fibre
20g Carbs
84 Cals
1 5-a-day

Grapefruit Juice
75ml

0g Protein
0g Fat
0g Fibre
6g Carbs
25 Cals
½ 5-a-day

Grapefruit Juice
150ml

1g Protein
0g Fat
0g Fibre
12g Carbs
50 Cals
1 5-a-day

Lemon Juice
15ml, ¼ lemon

0g Protein
0g Fat
0g Fibre
0g Carbs
1 Cals
0 5-a-day

Lemon Juice
30ml, ½ lemon

0g Protein
0g Fat
0g Fibre
0g Carbs
2 Cals
0 5-a-day

Lime Juice
10ml, 1/4 lime

0g Protein
0g Fat
0g Fibre
0g Carbs
1 Cals
0 5-a-day

Lime Juice
20ml, 1/2 lime

0g Protein
0g Fat
0g Fibre
0g Carbs
2 Cals
0 5-a-day

Orange Juice
75ml

0g Protein
0g Fat
0g Fibre
7g Carbs
27 Cals
1/2 5-a-day

Orange Juice
150ml

1g Protein
0g Fat
0g Fibre
13g Carbs
54 Cals
1 5-a-day

Pineapple Juice
75ml

0g Protein
0g Fat
0g Fibre
8g Carbs
31 Cals
1/2 5-a-day

Pineapple Juice
150ml

0g Protein
0g Fat
0g Fibre
16g Carbs
62 Cals
1 5-a-day

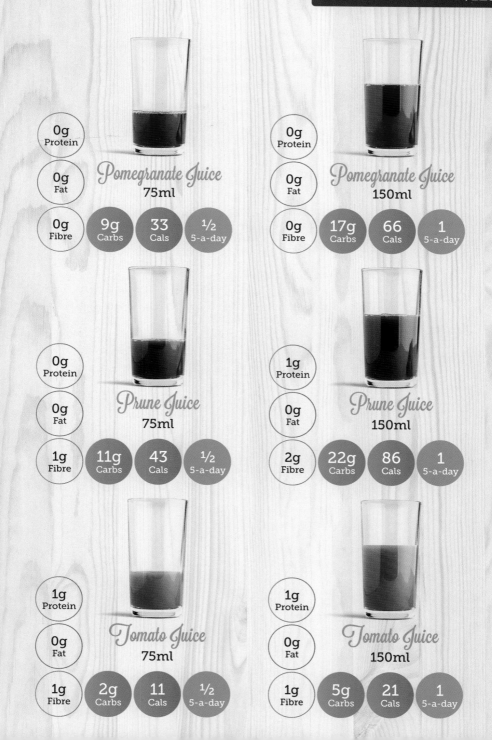

Pomegranate Juice
75ml

0g Protein
0g Fat
0g Fibre
9g Carbs
33 Cals
1/2 5-a-day

Pomegranate Juice
150ml

0g Protein
0g Fat
0g Fibre
17g Carbs
66 Cals
1 5-a-day

Prune Juice
75ml

0g Protein
0g Fat
1g Fibre
11g Carbs
43 Cals
1/2 5-a-day

Prune Juice
150ml

1g Protein
0g Fat
2g Fibre
22g Carbs
86 Cals
1 5-a-day

Tomato Juice
75ml

1g Protein
0g Fat
1g Fibre
2g Carbs
11 Cals
1/2 5-a-day

Tomato Juice
150ml

1g Protein
0g Fat
1g Fibre
5g Carbs
21 Cals
1 5-a-day

Coconut Water
100ml

0g Protein
0g Fat
0g Fibre
4g Carbs
17 Cals
0 5-a-day

Coconut Water
200ml

0g Protein
0g Fat
0g Fibre
9g Carbs
35 Cals
0 5-a-day

Espresso
60ml, double shot

0g Protein
0g Fat
0g Fibre
0g Carbs
1 Cals
0 5-a-day

Green Tea
100ml

0g Protein
0g Fat
0g Fibre
0g Carbs
0 Cals
0 5-a-day

Rose Water
5ml, 1 tsp

0g Protein
0g Fat
0g Fibre
0g Carbs
0 Cals
0 5-a-day

Vanilla Essence
a few drops

0g Protein
0g Fat
0g Fibre
0g Carbs
0 Cals
0 5-a-day

*Coconut Milk refers to the milk substitute, not tinned coconut milk (which is much more calorific!)

Almond Milk
100ml

1g Protein
1g Fat
0g Fibre
3g Carbs
24 Cals
0 5-a-day

Coconut Milk*
100ml

0g Protein
0g Fat
0g Fibre
5g Carbs
22 Cals
0 5-a-day

Goat's Milk
100ml

3g Protein
4g Fat
0g Fibre
4g Carbs
60 Cals
0 5-a-day

Hemp Milk
100ml

1g Protein
3g Fat
0g Fibre
3g Carbs
39 Cals
0 5-a-day

Oat Milk
100ml

1g Protein
1g Fat
1g Fibre
7g Carbs
46 Cals
0 5-a-day

Rice Milk
100ml

0g Protein
1g Fat
0g Fibre
10g Carbs
49 Cals
0 5-a-day

Milk (skimmed)
100ml

3g Protein
0g Fat
0g Fibre
4g Carbs
32 Cals
0 5-a-day

Milk (skimmed)
200ml

7g Protein
0g Fat
0g Fibre
9g Carbs
64 Cals
0 5-a-day

Milk (1%)
100ml

3g Protein
1g Fat
0g Fibre
5g Carbs
41 Cals
0 5-a-day

Milk (1%)
200ml

6g Protein
2g Fat
0g Fibre
9g Carbs
82 Cals
0 5-a-day

Milk (semi-skimmed)
100ml

3g Protein
2g Fat
0g Fibre
5g Carbs
46 Cals
0 5-a-day

Milk (semi-skimmed)
200ml

7g Protein
3g Fat
0g Fibre
9g Carbs
92 Cals
0 5-a-day

Milk (whole)
100ml

3g Protein
4g Fat
0g Fibre
5g Carbs
66 Cals
0 5-a-day

Milk (whole)
200ml

7g Protein
8g Fat
0g Fibre
9g Carbs
132 Cals
0 5-a-day

Soya Milk (sweetened)
100ml

3g Protein
2g Fat
1g Fibre
3g Carbs
43 Cals
0 5-a-day

Soya Milk (sweetened)
200ml

6g Protein
5g Fat
1g Fibre
5g Carbs
86 Cals
0 5-a-day

Soya Milk (unsweetened)
100ml

2g Protein
2g Fat
1g Fibre
1g Carbs
26 Cals
0 5-a-day

Soya Milk (unsweetened)
200ml

5g Protein
3g Fat
1g Fibre
1g Carbs
52 Cals
0 5-a-day

2g
Protein

6g
Fat

1g
Fibre

Almonds
10g, 1 tbsp

1g
Carbs

61
Cals

0
5-a-day

4g
Protein

11g
Fat

1g
Fibre

Almonds
20g, 2 tbsp

1g
Carbs

122
Cals

0
5-a-day

1g
Protein

7g
Fat

1g
Fibre

Brazil Nuts
10g, 1 tbsp

0g
Carbs

68
Cals

0
5-a-day

3g
Protein

14g
Fat

1g
Fibre

Brazil Nuts
20g, 2 tbsp

1g
Carbs

137
Cals

0
5-a-day

2g
Protein

5g
Fat

0g
Fibre

Cashews
10g, 1 tbsp

2g
Carbs

57
Cals

0
5-a-day

4g
Protein

10g
Fat

1g
Fibre

Cashews
20g, 2 tbsp

4g
Carbs

115
Cals

0
5-a-day

Hazelnuts
10g, 1 tbsp

1g Protein
6g Fat
1g Fibre
1g Carbs
65 Cals
0 5-a-day

Hazelnuts
20g, 2 tbsp

3g Protein
13g Fat
2g Fibre
1g Carbs
130 Cals
0 5-a-day

Macadamia Nuts
10g

1g Protein
8g Fat
1g Fibre
0g Carbs
75 Cals
0 5-a-day

Macadamia Nuts
20g

2g Protein
16g Fat
1g Fibre
1g Carbs
150 Cals
0 5-a-day

Peanuts
10g, 1 tbsp

3g Protein
5g Fat
1g Fibre
1g Carbs
56 Cals
0 5-a-day

Peanuts
20g, 2 tbsp

5g Protein
9g Fat
1g Fibre
3g Carbs
113 Cals
0 5-a-day

1g Protein
7g Fat
1g Fibre

Pecans
10g, 1 tbsp

1g Carbs
69 Cals
0 5-a-day

2g Protein
14g Fat
1g Fibre

Pecans
20g, 2 tbsp

1g Carbs
138 Cals
0 5-a-day

2g Protein
6g Fat
1g Fibre

Pistachios
10g, 1 tbsp

1g Carbs
60 Cals
0 5-a-day

4g Protein
11g Fat
2g Fibre

Pistachios
20g, 2 tbsp

2g Carbs
120 Cals
0 5-a-day

1g Protein
7g Fat
0g Fibre

Walnuts
10g, 1 tbsp

0g Carbs
69 Cals
0 5-a-day

3g Protein
14g Fat
1g Fibre

Walnuts
20g, 2 tbsp

1g Carbs
138 Cals
0 5-a-day

Chia Seeds
2g, ½ tsp

0g Protein
1g Fat
1g Fibre
0g Carbs
9 Cals
0 5-a-day

Chia Seeds
4g, 1 tsp

1g Protein
1g Fat
1g Fibre
0g Carbs
19 Cals
0 5-a-day

Hemp Seeds
10g, 1 tbsp

4g Protein
5g Fat
1g Fibre
1g Carbs
59 Cals
0 5-a-day

Hemp Seeds
20g, 2 tbsp

7g Protein
10g Fat
1g Fibre
2g Carbs
119 Cals
0 5-a-day

Linseeds
10g, 1 tbsp

2g Protein
4g Fat
3g Fibre
2g Carbs
50 Cals
0 5-a-day

Linseeds
20g, 2 tbsp

4g Protein
8g Fat
6g Fibre
4g Carbs
101 Cals
0 5-a-day

2g Protein
5g Fat
1g Fibre

Mixed Seeds
10g, 1 tbsp

1g Carbs · **59** Cals · **0** 5-a-day

5g Protein
10g Fat
2g Fibre

Mixed Seeds
20g, 2 tbsp

2g Carbs · **118** Cals · **0** 5-a-day

2g Protein
5g Fat
1g Fibre

Pumpkin Seeds
10g, 1 tbsp

2g Carbs · **57** Cals · **0** 5-a-day

5g Protein
9g Fat
1g Fibre

Pumpkin Seeds
20g, 2 tbsp

3g Carbs · **114** Cals · **0** 5-a-day

2g Protein
5g Fat
1g Fibre

Sunflower Seeds
10g, 1 tbsp

2g Carbs · **58** Cals · **0** 5-a-day

4g Protein
10g Fat
2g Fibre

Sunflower Seeds
20g, 2 tbsp

4g Carbs · **116** Cals · **0** 5-a-day

1g Protein			
0g Fat			
0g Fibre	1g Carbs	7 Cals	0 5-a-day

Cacao
2g, 1 tsp

2g Protein			
1g Fat			
2g Fibre	3g Carbs	25 Cals	0 5-a-day

Cacao
7g, 1 tbsp

0g Protein			
0g Fat			
0g Fibre	0g Carbs	0 Cals	0 5-a-day

Cinnamon
pinch

0g Protein			
0g Fat			
0g Fibre	0g Carbs	0 Cals	0 5-a-day

Nutmeg
pinch

2g Protein			
0g Fat			
0g Fibre	0g Carbs	10 Cals	0 5-a-day

Spirulina
3g, 1 tsp

7g Protein			
0g Fat			
1g Fibre	1g Carbs	34 Cals	0 5-a-day

Spirulina
10g, 1 tbsp

1g Protein			
0g Fat			
	Hemp Protein		
	3g, 1 tsp		
1g Fibre	1g Carbs	12 Cals	0 5-a-day

5g Protein			
1g Fat			
	Hemp Protein		
	10g, 1 tbsp		
2g Fibre	2g Carbs	39 Cals	0 5-a-day

0g Protein			
0g Fat			
	Wheatgrass		
	2g, 1 tsp		
1g Fibre	0g Carbs	5 Cals	0 5-a-day

1g Protein			
0g Fat			
	Wheatgrass		
	6g, 1 tbsp		
3g Fibre	1g Carbs	14 Cals	0 5-a-day

6g Protein			
0g Fat			
	Whey Protein		
	8g, 1 tbsp		
0g Fibre	1g Carbs	30 Cals	0 5-a-day

11g Protein			
1g Fat			
	Whey Protein		
	15g, 2 tbsp		
0g Fibre	1g Carbs	57 Cals	0 5-a-day

Almond Butter
5g, 1 tsp

1g Protein
3g Fat
1g Fibre
0g Carbs
33 Cals
0 5-a-day

Almond Butter
15g, 1 tbsp

4g Protein
8g Fat
2g Fibre
1g Carbs
98 Cals
0 5-a-day

Honey
6g, 1 tsp

0g Protein
0g Fat
0g Fibre
5g Carbs
17 Cals
0 5-a-day

Honey
18g, 1 tbsp

0g Protein
0g Fat
0g Fibre
14g Carbs
52 Cals
0 5-a-day

Jam
7g, 1 tsp

0g Protein
0g Fat
0g Fibre
4g Carbs
18 Cals
0 5-a-day

Jam
20g, 1 tbsp

0g Protein
0g Fat
0g Fibre
12g Carbs
52 Cals
0 5-a-day

Maple Syrup
6g, 1 tsp

0g Protein
0g Fat
0g Fibre
4g Carbs
16 Cals
0 5-a-day

Maple Syrup
17g, 1 tbsp

0g Protein
0g Fat
0g Fibre
11g Carbs
45 Cals
0 5-a-day

Peanut Butter
5g, 1 tsp

1g Protein
2g Fat
0g Fibre
1g Carbs
30 Cals
0 5-a-day

Peanut Butter
15g, 1 tbsp

4g Protein
7g Fat
1g Fibre
2g Carbs
91 Cals
0 5-a-day

Tahini
5g, 1 tsp

1g Protein
3g Fat
1g Fibre
0g Carbs
30 Cals
0 5-a-day

Tahini
15g, 1 tbsp

3g Protein
9g Fat
2g Fibre
0g Carbs
91 Cals
0 5-a-day

Asparagus Tips
40g

1g Protein	
0g Fat	
1g Fibre	1g Carbs · 10 Cals · ½ 5-a-day

Asparagus Tips
80g

2g Protein	
0g Fat	
2g Fibre	2g Carbs · 20 Cals · 1 5-a-day

Avocado
35g

1g Protein	
7g Fat	
2g Fibre	1g Carbs · 67 Cals · 0 5-a-day

Avocado
70g

1g Protein	
14g Fat	
3g Fibre	1g Carbs · 134 Cals · ½ 5-a-day

Beetroot
40g, small, boiled

1g Protein	
0g Fat	
1g Fibre	4g Carbs · 18 Cals · ½ 5-a-day

Beetroot
80g, 2 small, boiled

2g Protein	
0g Fat	
2g Fibre	8g Carbs · 37 Cals · 1 5-a-day

1g Protein

0g Fat

1g Fibre

Beetroot
40g, 1/2 medium, peeled

3g Carbs · 14 Cals · 1/2 5-a-day

1g Protein

0g Fat

2g Fibre

Beetroot
80g, peeled

6g Carbs · 29 Cals · 1 5-a-day

2g Protein

0g Fat

1g Fibre

Broccoli
40g

1g Carbs · 13 Cals · 1/2 5-a-day

4g Protein

1g Fat

3g Fibre

Broccoli
80g

1g Carbs · 26 Cals · 1 5-a-day

0g Protein

0g Fat

1g Fibre

Butternut Squash
40g, boiled

3g Carbs · 13 Cals · 1/2 5-a-day

1g Protein

0g Fat

2g Fibre

Butternut Squash
80g, boiled

6g Carbs · 26 Cals · 1 5-a-day

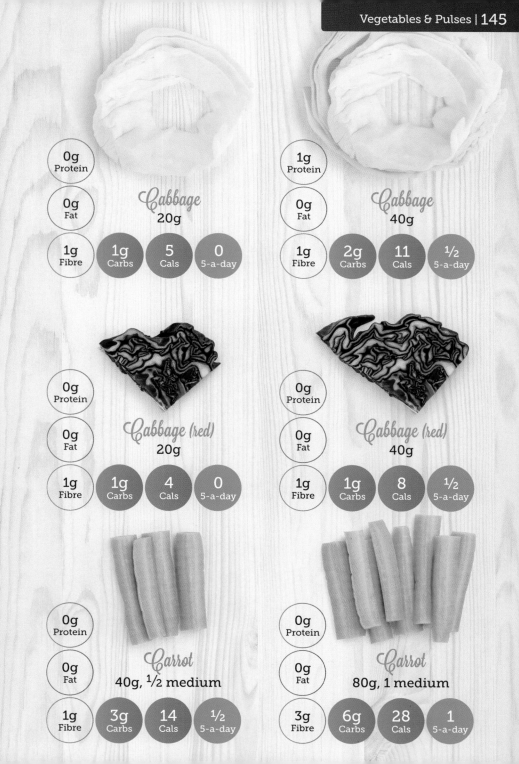

Cabbage
20g

- 0g Protein
- 0g Fat
- 1g Fibre
- 1g Carbs
- 5 Cals
- 0 5-a-day

Cabbage
40g

- 1g Protein
- 0g Fat
- 1g Fibre
- 2g Carbs
- 11 Cals
- ½ 5-a-day

Cabbage (red)
20g

- 0g Protein
- 0g Fat
- 1g Fibre
- 1g Carbs
- 4 Cals
- 0 5-a-day

Cabbage (red)
40g

- 0g Protein
- 0g Fat
- 1g Fibre
- 1g Carbs
- 8 Cals
- ½ 5-a-day

Carrot
40g, ½ medium

- 0g Protein
- 0g Fat
- 1g Fibre
- 3g Carbs
- 14 Cals
- ½ 5-a-day

Carrot
80g, 1 medium

- 0g Protein
- 0g Fat
- 3g Fibre
- 6g Carbs
- 28 Cals
- 1 5-a-day

1g Protein
0g Fat
1g Fibre

Cauliflower
40g

1g Carbs
14 Cals
½ 5-a-day

3g Protein
1g Fat
2g Fibre

Cauliflower
80g

2g Carbs
27 Cals
1 5-a-day

0g Protein
0g Fat
1g Fibre

Celery
40g

0g Carbs
3 Cals
½ 5-a-day

0g Protein
0g Fat
1g Fibre

Celery
80g

1g Carbs
6 Cals
1 5-a-day

0g Protein
0g Fat
1g Fibre

Cherry Tomatoes
40g, 4 small

1g Carbs
7 Cals
½ 5-a-day

1g Protein
0g Fat
1g Fibre

Cherry Tomatoes
80g, 8 small

2g Carbs
14 Cals
1 5-a-day

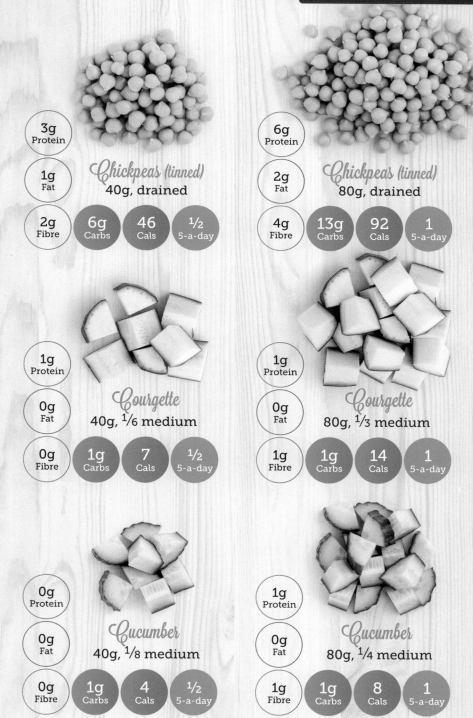

3g Protein

1g Fat

2g Fibre

Chickpeas (tinned)
40g, drained

6g Carbs | **46** Cals | **½** 5-a-day

6g Protein

2g Fat

4g Fibre

Chickpeas (tinned)
80g, drained

13g Carbs | **92** Cals | **1** 5-a-day

1g Protein

0g Fat

0g Fibre

Courgette
40g, ⅙ medium

1g Carbs | **7** Cals | **½** 5-a-day

1g Protein

0g Fat

1g Fibre

Courgette
80g, ⅓ medium

1g Carbs | **14** Cals | **1** 5-a-day

0g Protein

0g Fat

0g Fibre

Cucumber
40g, ⅛ medium

1g Carbs | **4** Cals | **½** 5-a-day

1g Protein

0g Fat

1g Fibre

Cucumber
80g, ¼ medium

1g Carbs | **8** Cals | **1** 5-a-day

Fennel
40g

0g Protein	0g Fat	1g Fibre

1g Carbs	5 Cals	½ 5-a-day

Fennel
80g

1g Protein	0g Fat	3g Fibre

1g Carbs	10 Cals	1 5-a-day

Green Beans
40g

1g Protein	0g Fat	1g Fibre

1g Carbs	10 Cals	½ 5-a-day

Green Beans
80g

2g Protein	0g Fat	2g Fibre

3g Carbs	19 Cals	1 5-a-day

Ginger
5g, 1 inch, peeled

0g Protein	0g Fat	0g Fibre

0g Carbs	2 Cals	0 5-a-day

Ginger
10g, 2 inches, peeled

0g Protein	0g Fat	0g Fibre

1g Carbs	5 Cals	0 5-a-day

Kale
20g, handful

1g Protein		
0g Fat		
1g Fibre	0g Carbs	7 Cals	0 5-a-day

Kale
40g, 2 handfuls

1g Protein		
1g Fat		
2g Fibre	1g Carbs	13 Cals	½ 5-a-day

Kidney Beans (tinned)
40g, drained

3g Protein		
0g Fat		
3g Fibre	7g Carbs	40 Cals	½ 5-a-day

Kidney Beans (tinned)
80g, drained

6g Protein		
0g Fat		
7g Fibre	14g Carbs	80 Cals	1 5-a-day

Lentils (tinned)
40g, drained

4g Protein		
0g Fat		
2g Fibre	7g Carbs	42 Cals	½ 5-a-day

Lentils (tinned)
80g, drained

7g Protein		
1g Fat		
4g Fibre	14g Carbs	84 Cals	1 5-a-day

0g
Protein

0g
Fat

0g
Fibre

Lambs Lettuce
20g, large handful

0g
Carbs

3
Cals

0
5-a-day

1g
Protein

0g
Fat

0g
Fibre

Lambs Lettuce
40g, 2 large handfuls

1g
Carbs

6
Cals

½
5-a-day

0g
Protein

0g
Fat

0g
Fibre

Lettuce
20g

0g
Carbs

3
Cals

0
5-a-day

0g
Protein

0g
Fat

0g
Fibre

Lettuce
40g

1g
Carbs

6
Cals

½
5-a-day

1g
Protein

0g
Fat

1g
Fibre

Mushrooms
40g

0g
Carbs

5
Cals

½
5-a-day

1g
Protein

0g
Fat

1g
Fibre

Mushrooms
80g

0g
Carbs

10
Cals

1
5-a-day

1g Protein
0g Fat
1g Fibre

Mangetout
40g

2g Carbs
13 Cals
½ 5-a-day

3g Protein
0g Fat
2g Fibre

Mangetout
80g

3g Carbs
26 Cals
1 5-a-day

1g Protein
0g Fat
3g Fibre

Parsnip
40g, boiled

5g Carbs
26 Cals
½ 5-a-day

1g Protein
1g Fat
5g Fibre

Parsnip
80g, boiled

10g Carbs
53 Cals
1 5-a-day

2g Protein
0g Fat
3g Fibre

Peas
40g

4g Carbs
28 Cals
½ 5-a-day

5g Protein
1g Fat
5g Fibre

Peas
80g

8g Carbs
55 Cals
1 5-a-day

Pepper
40g, ¼ small

0g Protein
0g Fat
1g Fibre
2g Carbs
10 Cals
½ 5-a-day

Pepper
80g, ½ small

1g Protein
0g Fat
2g Fibre
4g Carbs
21 Cals
1 5-a-day

Rhubarb (tinned)
40g

0g Protein
0g Fat
0g Fibre
3g Carbs
12 Cals
½ 5-a-day

Rhubarb (tinned)
80g

0g Protein
0g Fat
1g Fibre
6g Carbs
25 Cals
1 5-a-day

Soya Beans
40g

5g Protein
3g Fat
2g Fibre
2g Carbs
56 Cals
½ 5-a-day

Soya Beans
80g

10g Protein
5g Fat
3g Fibre
3g Carbs
113 Cals
1 5-a-day

Spinach
20g, handful

1g Protein
0g Fat
1g Fibre
0g Carbs
5 Cals
0 5-a-day

Spinach
40g, 2 handfuls

1g Protein
0g Fat
1g Fibre
1g Carbs
10 Cals
½ 5-a-day

Sugar Snap Peas
40g

1g Protein
0g Fat
1g Fibre
2g Carbs
14 Cals
½ 5-a-day

Sugar Snap Peas
80g

3g Protein
0g Fat
2g Fibre
4g Carbs
27 Cals
1 5-a-day

Sweetcorn
40g

1g Protein
0g Fat
1g Fibre
11g Carbs
49 Cals
½ 5-a-day

Sweetcorn
80g

2g Protein
1g Fat
2g Fibre
21g Carbs
98 Cals
1 5-a-day

0g Protein

0g Fat

1g Fibre

Sweet Potato
40g, ¼ small, boiled

8g Carbs | **34** Cals | **½** 5-a-day

1g Protein

0g Fat

2g Fibre

Sweet Potato
80g, ½ small, boiled

16g Carbs | **67** Cals | **1** 5-a-day

0g Protein

0g Fat

1g Fibre

Tomato
40g, small

1g Carbs | **7** Cals | **½** 5-a-day

1g Protein

0g Fat

1g Fibre

Tomato
80g, 2 small

2g Carbs | **14** Cals | **1** 5-a-day

1g Protein

0g Fat

0g Fibre

Watercress
20g, large handful

0g Carbs | **4** Cals | **0** 5-a-day

1g Protein

0g Fat

1g Fibre

Watercress
40g, 2 large handfuls

0g Carbs | **9** Cals | **½** 5-a-day

4g Protein

0g Fat

0g Fibre

Greek Yogurt (fat-free)
50g

3g Carbs | **27** Cals | **0** 5-a-day

7g Protein

0g Fat

0g Fibre

Greek Yogurt (fat-free)
100g

5g Carbs | **54** Cals | **0** 5-a-day

3g Protein

0g Fat

0g Fibre

Natural Yogurt (fat-free)
50g

4g Carbs | **27** Cals | **0** 5-a-day

6g Protein

0g Fat

0g Fibre

Natural Yogurt (fat-free)
100g

7g Carbs | **54** Cals | **0** 5-a-day

2g Protein

1g Fat

1g Fibre

Soya Yogurt
50g

1g Carbs | **25** Cals | **0** 5-a-day

4g Protein

2g Fat

1g Fibre

Soya Yogurt
100g

2g Carbs | **50** Cals | **0** 5-a-day

Smoothie Index

Acid Raspberries 28
Almond Amore 59
Almond Cheer 74
Avofennel Fusion 56
Beetroot Brekkie 101
Berry Velvety 94
Bittersweet Rose 85
Blue Ginger 30
Burgundy Zinger 82
Carbs & Cals Waldorf 105
Carrot Classic 41
Carrot & Cucumber Cooler 37
Cherry Afters 67
Choco Orange Date 60
Choco Tropical 63
Chris's Cauli 79
Citrus Rooter 44
Cocopineapple Cooler 45
Cream of Mango 62
Cucumelon Rose 29
Cup o' Cacao 71
Double Coconut 93
Espresso Date 75
Figgin' Sweet 70
Fruit Pod 88
Grapefruit Froth 35
Grass in a Glass 92
Great Greens 86
Hannah Banana 69
Hello Yello 64
Hempy Vegan 103
Hey Pesto! 31
Kale Kerfuffle 43
Kiwi Kicker 83
Kiwi Spotlight 58
Kiwi Yoshi 50
Lettuce Be 77
Love it or Hate it! 38
Lychee Tea 34
Mandarin Cream 61

Mango Tango 39
Melon Mayhem! 80
Melon Quencher 33
Melon Salad 78
Milkless Milkshake 48
Morning Glory 106
Muesli in the Morning 97
Multi Mix-up 81
Nuts & Whey 102
Oaty Cinny 100
Orangetastic 46
Parsnip Badger 90
Passionately Green 40
Passion for Prunes 89
Peachy Hazels 73
Peanut Butter Cup 107
Pear Aplomb 51
Pear of Blueberries 32
Pick up a Pepper 53
Planting a Seed 99
Pomegranate Greek 98
Protein Powershake 104
Raspberry Ripple 54
Ready Racer 96
Rosie Rhubarb 52
Satin Berry Smooth 91
Seedy Satsuma 72
Shady Spinach 55
Speckled Melon 47
Strawberry Barb 84
Summer Zing 57
Sweet Beet 87
Sweet Potato Tang 49
Sweet Thyme 65
Tarty Blast 42
The Apricotty 95
The Naughty Cup 76
Toffee Apple 68
Vanilla Date Shake 66
Watermelon Mary 36

Ingredients Index

A

Almond Butter 141
Almond Milk 59, 63, 65, 73, 74, 77, 97, 104, 131
Almonds 75, 134
Apple 112
    Green 43, 52, 65, 68, 69, 86, 105
    Juice 126
    Red 41, 46, 50, 51, 72, 79, 84, 92, 100
    Rings (dried) 87, 109
Apricots 64, 83, 93, 112
    (dried) 73, 95, 109
Asparagus 78, 143
Avocado 53, 56, 86, 92, 103, 143

B

Banana 55, 59, 61, 63, 64, 65, 66, 67, 69, 70, 72, 74, 75, 76, 77, 83, 90, 94, 96, 102, 103, 104, 106, 107, 112
Basil 31, 36, 125
Beans 148, 149, 152
Beetroot
    (boiled) 82, 101, 143
    Juice 126
    (raw) 44, 87, 93, 144
Blackberries 88, 91, 100, 113
Black Forest Fruit (frozen) 99
Blueberries 30, 32, 55, 58, 59, 69, 74, 81, 96, 98, 103, 113
    (frozen) 87, 89, 100, 123
Bran 96, 108
Brazil Nuts 134
Broccoli 78, 86, 144
Butternut Squash 144

C

Cabbage 145
    Red 82, 87, 145

Cacao Powder 60, 63, 66, 67, 71, 102, 139
Cantaloupe 29, 80, 113
Carrot 37, 41, 44, 46, 78, 79, 81, 82, 87, 90, 106, 145
    Juice 126
Cashews 77, 134
Cauliflower 78, 79, 146
Celery 31, 41, 43, 53, 78, 81, 146
Cherries 73, 114
    (frozen) 67, 123
Cherry Tomatoes 146
Chia Seeds 56, 66, 74, 89, 137
Chickpeas 147
Chocolate 38 (see also Cacao)
Cinnamon 66, 68, 71, 77, 100, 139
Coconut 93, 97, 104, 114
    Milk 63, 95, 131
    Water 38, 45, 47, 52, 55, 58, 62, 65, 85, 93, 102, 130
Coriander 125
Courgette 31, 43, 78, 86, 147
Cranberries (dried) 107, 109
Cranberry Juice 127
Cucumber 29, 31, 36, 37, 50, 55, 78, 79, 81, 106, 147

D

Dark Chocolate 38
Dates 60, 66, 75, 76, 103, 110
    Medjool 68

E

Espresso 75, 130

F

Fennel 56, 79, 148
Figs 114
    (dried) 70, 74, 91, 104, 110

G

Galia Melon 29, 33, 78, 80, 115
Ginger 30, 44, 46, 62, 79, 80, 89, 148
Goat's Milk 131
Goji Berries (dried) 42, 110
Grapefruit 35, 49, 85, 115
　Juice 127
Grapes 48, 81, 88, 106, 115
Greek Yogurt 62, 98, 106, 155
Green Beans 148
Green Tea 34, 89, 130

H

Hazelnuts 73, 135
Hemp
　Milk 66, 131
　Protein Powder 95, 103, 140
　Seeds 137
Honey 65, 96, 141
Honeydew Melon 80, 83, 116

J

Jam 141

K

Kale 31, 40, 43, 59, 86, 89, 92, 102, 149
Kidney Beans 149
Kiwi 42, 50, 52, 58, 69, 83, 99, 116

L

Lambs Lettuce 31, 150
Lemon 82, 116
　Juice 30, 31, 36, 42, 43, 78, 127
Lentils 149
Lettuce 31, 77, 78, 150
Lime 28, 32, 50, 62, 81, 117
　Juice 30, 32, 33, 38, 39, 42, 53, 56, 79, 92, 128
Linseeds 137
Lychees 34, 84, 117

M

Macadamia Nuts 135
Mandarin 61, 83, 85, 117
Mangetout 151
Mango 39, 40, 50, 57, 58, 64, 70, 84, 88, 93, 95, 106, 118
　(frozen) 62, 85, 123
Maple Syrup 54, 105, 142
Medjool Dates 68
Melon
　Cantaloupe 29, 80, 113
　Galia 29, 33, 78, 80, 115
　Honeydew 80, 83, 116
　Watermelon 33, 36, 50, 55, 58, 70, 71, 80, 122
Milk 60, 67, 100, 105, 132–133
　Almond 59, 63, 65, 73, 74, 77, 97, 104, 131
　Coconut 63, 95, 131
　Goat's 131
　Hemp 66, 131
　Oat 54, 96, 107, 131
　Rice 131
　Soya 71, 75, 76, 94, 103, 133
Mint 33, 34, 42, 62, 78, 125
Mixed Berries (frozen) 57, 99, 101, 106, 124
Mixed Seeds 72, 99, 138
Muesli 97, 101, 106, 108
Mushrooms 150

N

Natural Yogurt 91, 99, 100, 101, 105, 155
Nectarine 118
Nutmeg 66, 139

O

Oat
　Bran 96, 108
　Milk 54, 96, 107, 131
Oats 100, 107, 108
Orange 37, 44, 46, 49, 57, 60, 65, 80, 82, 85, 87, 88, 101, 118
　Juice 128

P

Papaya 59, 119
Parsley 43, 86, 92, 125
Parsnip 90, 151
Passion Fruit 40, 47, 89, 119
Peach 73, 88, 119
Peanut Butter 76, 102, 107, 142
Peanuts 135
Pear 32, 51, 53, 65, 70, 81, 82, 92, 120
Peas 151
   Sugar Snap 153
Pecans 136
Pepper 53, 152
Persimmon 120
Pineapple 35, 47, 48, 57, 62, 63, 64, 72, 81, 82, 83, 85, 87, 90, 95, 120
   (frozen) 45, 56, 86, 124
   Juice 128
Pistachios 71, 136
Plums 51, 64, 81, 121
Pomegranate
   Juice 129
   Seeds 96, 98, 121
Protein Powder
   Hemp 95, 103, 140
   Whey 102, 104, 140
Prune Juice 129
Prunes 89, 94, 111
Pumpkin Seeds 106, 138

R

Raisins 71, 77, 87, 97, 111
Raspberries 81, 88, 89, 91, 94, 97, 103, 121
   (frozen) 28, 54, 98, 124
Red Cabbage 82, 87, 145
Rhubarb 52, 84, 152
Rice Milk 131
Rosemary 52, 125
Rose Water 29, 68, 85, 130

S

Satsuma 72, 122
Soya
   Beans 152
   Milk 71, 75, 76, 94, 103, 133
   Yogurt 61, 155
Spinach 31, 42, 50, 53, 55, 72, 82, 83, 86, 106, 153
Spirulina Powder 139
Strawberries 34, 41, 48, 74, 80, 81, 84, 85, 94, 99, 102, 122
Sugar Snap Peas 153
Sultanas 105, 111
Summer Fruit (frozen) 57, 101, 106, 124
Sunflower Seeds 107, 138
Sweetcorn 153
Sweet Potato 49, 77, 154

T

Tahini 142
Thyme 65, 125
Tomato 36, 38, 154
   Cherry 146
   Juice 129

V

Vanilla
   Essence 66, 95, 130
   Pod 88

W

Walnuts 105, 136
Watercress 154
Watermelon 33, 36, 47, 50, 55, 58, 70, 71, 80, 122
Wheatgrass Powder 86, 140
Whey Protein 102, 104, 140

Y

Yogurt
   Greek 62, 98, 106, 155
   Natural 91, 100, 101, 105, 155
   Soya 61, 155

About the Authors

Chris Cheyette BSc (Hons) MSc RD
Diabetes Specialist Dietitian

Chris is a Diabetes Specialist Dietitian within the NHS, working with people with type 1, type 2 and gestational diabetes. Chris has spearheaded a number of projects over the years, many with the aim of improving diabetes educational resources. These include an educational DVD for young people with diabetes, which earned him the 2007 British Dietetic Association Elizabeth Washington Award. Chris has also published a number of journal articles on weight management and diabetes. He regularly undertakes local and national presentations to healthcare professionals, has done TV & newspaper interviews, and has participated as a guest expert in online discussions.

Yello Balolia BA (Hons)
Entrepreneur & Creative Photographer

Having achieved a first class honours degree in Photography, Canada-born, Blackpool-bred and now London-based Yello used his entrepreneurial and creative skills to found Chello Publishing Limited with Chris Cheyette, to publish Carbs & Cals (**www.carbsandcals.com**), the bestselling and multi-award-winning book and app for diabetes and weight management. He has also undertaken a series of creative projects including private commissions (**www.yellobalolia.com**) and, as a keen musician, Yello recently set up Ukulology - a visual and effective way of learning the ukulele (**www.ukulology.com**).

Awards

Carbs & Cals won **Best Dietary Management Initiative** at the Quality in Care Awards 2014

The Carbs & Cals App won **New Product of the Year** in the Complete Nutrition Awards 2012

Carbs & Cals won the BDA Dame Barbara Clayton **Award for Innovation & Excellence** 2011

WINNER
QiC
Category: **Best Dietary Management Initiative**

Quality in Care Programme 2014

BDA
The Association of UK Dietitians

Winner of the 2011 Dame Barbara Clayton Award

Carbs & Cals APP
WINNER
NEW PRODUCT OF THE YEAR
CN awards

Carbs & Cals